Acting Games

IMPROVISATIONS AND EXERCISES

Marsh Cassady 1936

MERIWETHER PUBLISHING LTD.
Colorado Springs, Colorado

Meriwether Publishing Ltd., Publisher
Box 7710
Colorado Springs, CO 80933

Editor: Theodore O. Zapel
Typesetting: Sharon E. Garlock
Cover design: Tom Myers

© Copyright MCMXCIII Meriwether Publishing Ltd.
Printed in the United States of America
First Edition

Library of Congress Cataloging-in-Publication Data

Cassady, Marsh, 1936 -
    Acting games : improvisations and exercises / by Marsh Cassady. --
1st ed.
        p.   cm.
    ISBN 0-916260-92-5
    1. Improvisation (Acting) -- Juvenile literature. [1. Acting.]
I. Title.
PN2071.I5C28   1993
792--dc20   93-37322
                                                                  CIP
                                                                  AC

        4   5   6   7   8   9   99   98

To Jackie Ball

ACKNOWLEDGEMENTS

Excerpts from:

"An Iffy Situation," *Buckeye Country Magazine,* Winter, 1977; "When Benny Came to Town," *Triple Fiction,* Los Hombres Press, 1990; *Death by Stages,* novel in progress; "White Noise;" "Fitting the Mold," in slightly different form in *Love Theme With Variations,* Los Hombres Press, 1989; "Are You Happy?" "Dana and the Monster," in slightly different form in *Candle,* May, 1986; "The Beautiful Dress;" *Sounding Brass,* a novel in progress; "The Vow," *Triple Fiction,* Los Hombres Press, 1990; "Going Steady;" "The Magic Cheese" — all by Marsh Cassady. Reprinted by permission of the author.

The script of "Vampire" by Marsh Cassady. Reprinted by permission of the author.

The script of "Market" by Betty J. Reeves. Reprinted by permission of the author.

Excerpts from:

"The Camp Robber" by Herbert M. Kulman. Used by permission of the author.

"Coffee Cure-All" by Nirmala Moorthy. First excerpted in the *Times* of India. Used by permission of the author. "White Christmas" by Scott Myrom. Used by permission of the author. "Hate Child" by Art Specht. Used by permission of the author. "The Laughter" by Anne James Valades. Used by permission of the author.

PHOTO CREDITS

The Lion in Winter directed and designed by Mary Sesak, Heidelberg College, Tiffin, Ohio. Photo by Jeff McIntosh and used by his permission.

Long Day's Journey Into Night, directed by Bedford Thurman. Photo by James Gleason and used by permission of Kent State University.

A Thurber Carnival, designed by Rich Jagunic and directed by Marsh Cassady. Photo by Bill Douds and used by permission of Little Theatre of Tuscarawas County (Ohio).

The first set of wedding pictures used by permission of Beth Porterfield; the second set used by permission of Kim Smith.

Other photos used by permission of the models: David Cassady, Heather Cassady, Christopher Galea, Jim Kitchen, David Kitchen for Samantha Kitchen, Paul Kitchen, Herb Kulman, Kathi and Jeff McIntosh, James Palmer, Currie Silver. Additional models included were actors and associates of Contemporary Drama Service who have posed for photo illustrations of the many plays published by Contemporary Drama Service in Downers Grove, Illinois and Colorado Springs, Colorado.

Special thanks to Michael LaRochelle of Dean's Photo.

Drawings by Lue Sinclair, used by permission of Los Hombres Press; drawings by Gene Gryniewicz, used by permission of the artist.

TABLE OF CONTENTS

Introduction

The purpose of this book is to develop your creative abilities and talents in acting. The exercises are designed to lead you gradually from simple and enjoyable games through exercises aimed at building and portraying characters and scenes.

The book is divided into four sections that progress from simple exercises to those that require more planning and practice. As you go through the sections, you will receive help in becoming a more creative actor. But as important as anything else, remember that the exercises should be fun.

PART I

The first section includes games for relaxing and focusing. When you are relaxed, your energy levels are at their highest, allowing you to focus more completely on creating a scene or character.

Games for relaxing and focusing can and should become a regular part of any actor's preparation for a role or a performance.

This section ends with activities that do not take a lot of planning. Even though they do require focus and quick thinking, their main purpose is to ease you gently toward games that require more planning and elaboration.

PART II

The second section will teach new ways of looking at self, others and the world as a whole. Once you realize not only that it is possible, but that it is easy to change your views of the world, you are well on the way to being more creative.

Everyone has the ability to create. Some learn by themselves to tune into their creativity. Others do not, because as children, all of us have been taught to conform — to sit at desks and do what everyone else is doing, to "pay attention" and not cause problems. So as youngsters, people begin to think that being different or creative is wrong, and so they suppress this part of themselves. The activities in Part II can help you to get more in touch with your creativity.

PART III

The third section begins by showing how space can be used

effectively in building scenes and characters. It also includes improvisations to help develop situations, scenes and characters through observing others and figuring out their traits and characteristics.

PART IV

The activities in the final section involve analyzing and playing specific characters which you create or which come from already existing plays.

USING THE BOOK

Acting Games, Improvisations and Exercises gives much more space to activities rather than text. This is because a person learns to be creative and to act by "doing."

As you try each activity, remember that first of all you should have fun, which in this class should be your most important goal. The rest will follow naturally.

The book will not deal with the basics of acting. It will not contain lengthy discussions of voice usage or methods of approaching a role. These things are for an acting textbook.

The choosing of activities for each category is arbitrary. Many could fit into two or more categories. This means that you do not have to go from the front of the book to the back. Once you are acquainted with relaxing/focusing exercises, for instance, it is a good idea to use them to open every session. This is so you will be ready to "get to work" on more exacting activities later in the session.

You can jump around in the book, approaching the activities in whatever order you want. But unless you already have a background in acting and improvisation, you probably should not jump immediately into Section IV. It does require some knowledge and preparation.

APPROACHING THE ACTIVITIES

There are several important "rules" to keep in mind about theatre games. First, unless the activity calls for it, do not ramble. Try to build to a satisfactory ending. Second, you really have to pay attention to what the other actors do and say so that you can respond to them in a logical manner suited to the intention of the activity. Above all, stay on the subject and try to treat the situation as "real," no matter how silly or outrageous it seems.

SOME BASICS OF THEATRE

Many of the activities do not require a stage. But you still should keep in mind a few rules of performing in front of an audience. There are various body positions, some of which are better than others. Facing full front, of course, calls most attention to itself. But if you are sharing the performance area with others, this may not be practical. The following diagram shows the different body positions. The higher the number, the less desirable the position. Unless there is a good reason, for instance, you should not turn your back to your audience.

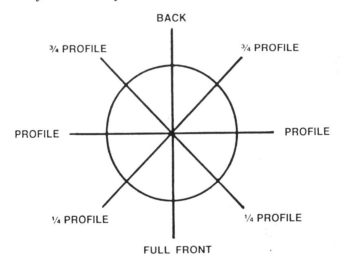

A stage can be divided into the following areas with upstage closest to the back wall, and downstage closest to the audience.

UR UP RIGHT	UC UP CENTER	UL UP LEFT
RC RIGHT CENTER	C CENTER	LC LEFT CENTER
DR DOWN RIGHT	DC DOWN CENTER	DL DOWN LEFT

3

When you kneel in profile, use your downstage knee, so you do not block your body. But use your upstage arm for the same reason. Another rule is that when you cross the playing area, it usually is best to use a gentle curve, so that you do not end up in an awkward position in relation to the audience.

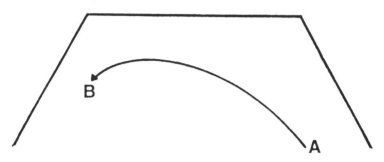

You may be wondering why you should do theatre games and improvisations.

One reason is that these activities involve you immediately in theatre without having to go to auditions, learn lines, and spend hours learning blocking (movement). Besides, they teach the need to watch, listen, and pay attention, rather than just to stare and wait, as actors unfortunately do sometimes in a play.

The kind of activities included in the book allow you to get in touch with your feelings and to look more deeply at the world around you. You can then bring what you learn to the activities and later, if you wish, to acting or directing plays. Some of the activities can be used concurrently with playing a role in a drama. These, of course, include the relaxation and focusing exercises. But more than that, you can do improvisations with your own character from a play to better understand him or her.

Of course, there are some acting groups that do only improvisational theatre, and there are people who do only pantomimes, such as the famous French mime Marcel Marceau. The book will certainly acquaint you with both these areas.

Theatre games and improvisations can give you confidence and help eliminate stage fright. If you can do these activities *without* a script, you certainly can then perform *with* a script.

The games and improvisations do not require long rehearsals and planning, which means that everyone gets a turn at doing all sorts of things — playing different roles and situations and learning to use the imagination.

The activities in the book should give you ideas for developing further games and improvisations. You do not need to be bound by what is included in the book. Feel free to come up with your own exercises for each of the categories.

The activities in the book can be performed in nearly any type of space — a classroom, a gym, or a stage. You do not even need much in the way of furniture or properties. It is a good idea if you have a few chairs that can be moved around, and a table and desk. Occasionally, you will be asked to bring objects from home. Or if you have access to your school's property room, that will often do just as well or better.

If for any reason it is awkward or impossible to perform any of the physical exercises in the first section, feel free to sit them out or to do those exercises you know you are physically capable of doing.

Have fun!

Part I:

RELAXING AND FOCUSING EXERCISES

Warming Up

In order to do your best creative work, you need to relax, to rid yourself of both mental and physical tension. The more relaxed your mind and body, the more easily you can devote all your attention to something else.

It's a good idea to do relaxation exercises any time before appearing in front of an audience. If you're especially tense, worried or tired, you may need to do more exercises than otherwise. It's like a runner loosening up before a race.

You'll probably find both physical and mental exercises that you like best. Those that follow are by no means the only ones that work or even the best for each person.

There's no need to do every one of these exercises every day. They're not an end in themselves but instead are to help prepare you for further exercises and activities. Once you stretch out the kinks and feel your body relax, you don't need to go on. The same is true with the mental exercises; do two or three a day until you feel you are in a frame of mind that allows you to do your best work.

PHYSICAL RELAXATION

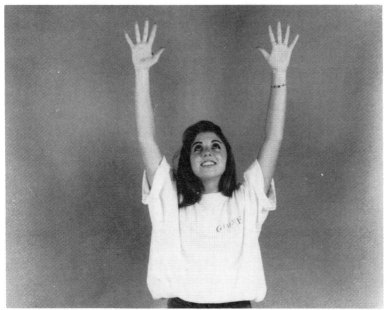

1. Stand with your legs 15 or 18 inches apart. Now reach straight up, stretching your arms as far as you can toward the sun. If you can't reach it, stand on tiptoes and use all your strength to stretch further. Then drop your feet flat on the floor and let your body sag forward, bending at the waist.

The next two exercises are to help you get rid of tension in your shoulders and neck, places where people often feel tense.

2. Imagine your arms are ropes, uncoiled at the ends to form your fingers. Let them hang loose at your sides and then shake them. As you do, allow any tension you feel in your shoulders and neck to flow down your arms and through your wrists to the ends of your fingers. Shake away the tension.

3. Standing with legs apart, let your head hang down, your chin on your chest. Now roll your head the entire way around, first to the right then to the left. Do this only a few times or you may start to feel dizzy. If you do, stop the exercise.

4. This is similar to the neck roll. Again stand with your legs apart. Hunch up your shoulders and then move them forward and around in a shoulder roll. Repeat this. Then reverse the direction.

5. Place your hands an inch or two apart on the back of your neck. Now massage your neck up and down and in circles.

6. Lie flat on your back. Feel in your mind each part of your body and think about its functions and purpose and how all the parts fit together. Imagine their separate vibrations. Now harmonize these vibrations until you feel them all working together to give you strength.

7. Stand and lean bracing yourself with your hands against the wall or hold onto something solid, such as a railing or a heavy piece of furniture. Then stretch one leg in back and the other in front, bent at the knee. Rock gently back and forth. Now switch the leg in front with the one in back and do the same thing, as shown in the photo on page 11.

8. Yawn and stretch your arms and arch your back.

9. Here are some exercises that are simply to help you limber up.

   a. Stand with your legs apart. Place your hands on your hips. Bend at the waist, first to the right and then to the left. Continue until you have completed five side-to-side bends.

   b. Stand with your feet close together. Lift your left leg and hug your knee, pulling it tightly against your chest. Do this with the right leg. Do both legs two or three times.

   c. Again, stand with your feet fairly close together. Bend your left leg backwards at the knee. Grab your left foot near the toes and bend it till the heel touches your body. Do the same thing with the right leg and foot. Do both legs two or three times.

11

10. This exercise is both physical and mental. Its purpose is to get you into the proper frame of mind and well on the way to a relaxed body. Lie on the floor in a spread eagle position, arms straight out from your shoulders, legs spread. Now arch your back a few times and stretch your arms and legs as far as you can. Keeping the same position, imagine that you are a five-pointed star drawing in the energy of the universe at each of the five points.

After a minute or two, when your entire being tingles and snaps with energy, stand up and prepare for another exercise.

11. Cup each hand and turn them so the right palm faces the left. Concentrate on the tips of your fingers vibrating with energy. Let the energy flow from hand to hand.

Choose a partner and have that person face away from you. Run both your hands, still cupped, up and down the person's back without really touching it, as shown in the photo on page 13.

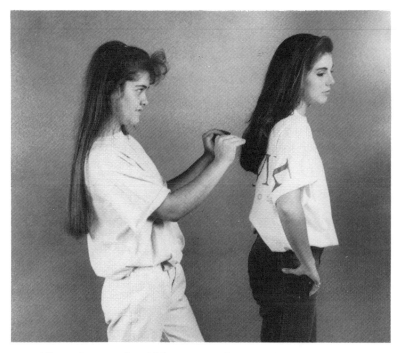

Your fingers should be two to three inches away from your partner. Imagine the energy flowing from your fingers into the person's shoulders and neck and back, easing away the tension. There's a name for this; it is called Touch Therapy.

Change places; now your partner will do the same thing, transferring energy to you.

12. This exercise is to make you feel a part of the whole. With your classmates, form a circle lying on the floor on your backs, feet toward the center, nearly touching the feet of the others. Stretch out your right and left hands till you can grasp the hands of those on either side of you. Concentrate on being a part of the circle. Remember that you're not alone but are part of the whole. Every part of the circle, every person there, like you, has worries and concerns. Draw energy and strength from each other. Concentrate on the energy flowing from others' hands into yours. Your own energy is different from theirs; it's what they need to feel fresh and relaxed. Exchange your energy for theirs the whole way around the circle. Each person's energy is flowing both right and left, making an almost visible band, crackling and snapping around and around the circle. Now release the

13

others' hands, relax for a second or two and stand up.

13. Try to come up with exercises of your own to help you relax or get rid of tension. Plan them out and share them with others, telling them how to do each one.

A different class member should be responsible each day for leading the group in exercises, for five to ten minutes, either those written here, those the leader comes up with, or a combination. Your teacher or one of you should prepare a sign-up sheet by date to make sure each person gets to lead the class at least one time.

MENTAL RELAXATION

Not only should you be relaxed before acting or improvising, but you should be focused as well. It's a common experience to perform everyday tasks, hardly being aware of it, like traveling somewhere and not remembering the route. Your mind concentrates on other things, or else you daydream. This is a good thing because it prevents boredom.

Yet when you act or do pantomimes or improvisations, you need to be able to focus in completely on what you are doing. To accomplish this, you need to push worries and concerns, and minor aches and pains back into a corner of your mind and focus on the task at hand. If you are tense or anxious, it means you are thinking more of self than about doing theatre games or improvisations.

While you are focused on what you are doing, you should open yourself to images and ideas without squelching them. This is sometimes difficult because as children you are taught to "be good," or to sit quietly and not disturb others. That's fine for some situations. But when you want to do anything creative, such as acting or playing theatre games, you need to learn to pay attention to your thoughts and feelings without censoring them or without thinking you have to conform or do just as others are doing. You need to be able to create freely without worrying about pleasing others.

That's why throughout the book you'll be given reminders not to laugh *at* (It's okay to laugh with them) others, not to be judgmental about what they do, but rather to create a place away from the everyday world that makes people conform by mocking them.

Although you can have freedom to do things your way in this

class, there still are certain rules you have to follow — like staying in the playing area and in most cases not turning your back on an audience. Other than that, playing theatre games is an individual thing. Each person does it differently because each looks at the world differently. It's important for you to realize that it's okay to experiment, to do things in your own way.

The exercises that follow, and others that are similar, help you to do that. Except for Exercise #3, which you need to take a few minutes to do by yourself, you can either imagine your way through each exercise or, much better, allow your teacher or a classmate to read the exercises slowly and with a lot of pauses to give you time to visualize and imagine all the details.

The purpose of each exercise is to put you in a creative frame of mind so you can 1) feel free to experiment, 2) change the way you think, and 3) realize that at least in the matter of theatre games, you don't have to think or behave as everyone else does.

1. Imagine that you are a balloon slowly filling with air as you breathe in. Take in more air and more and more until you fill your classroom, your town or city, your county, your state, your country, stretching up, feeling and imagining yourself growing bigger and bigger. Along the way look down at the countryside far below.

Once you have touched the moon, let your breath out slowly, shrinking, shrinking, shrinking till you fill your city, your classroom, your body.

2. For this exercise, you are to travel through your own bloodstream from the top of your head to the bottom of your feet. Enter at any place you wish and flow along all the canals and branches. Take with you a purifying agent that restores energy at the same time it rids the body of aches and pains. Shoot out puffs of the purifier all along the way. When your journey is complete, exit at the same point you entered, relaxed and filled with energy.

3. Think of a word, maybe your own name or something else that has a pleasant sound. Sit or lie in a relaxed position. Think only of the word and block out all worries and concerns. Repeat it over and over until only you and the word exist. Your teacher will call you back when it is time to go on.

15

One way of relaxing is to transport yourself mentally to soothing environments where you can almost feel the tension drain from your body.

4. Lie on your back, then draw your legs up and clasp your arms around your knees. Gently rock back and forth imagining:

    a. You are a thistle seed blown back and forth in a gentle breeze.

    b. In a few moments become instead a leaf floating lightly down a slow-moving stream. You have to make no effort either physically or mentally; the soothing water will do it for you.

    c. Now become a round pebble on the bottom of a shallow stream, being pushed back and forth, back and forth by eddies in the current.

5. Again become a thistle seed that is floating, floating through columns of air, the sun high up in a cloudless sky bathing you in a warming glow.

The gentle motion of the breeze lulls you as it carries you over mountains and towns. Ahead is an island covered in lush grass and tall, leafy trees. Near the edge of the island, you see a beach covered with sand. Slowly, slowly, the breeze gently sets you down. Lie there for a time enjoying the feel of the sand and the sounds of the lapping water, resuming your human form. Stand then and walk up the beach and explore the island. There's no hurry, nothing you have to do, nowhere you have to be. After you've circled the island, sit down, your back against the trunk of a shady tree. In a moment, a squirrel scurries through the trees and stops a few feet away.

It feeds on seeds and nuts and then joyfully scampers away. Lie back on a grassy mound, arms clasped behind your head, knowing no one can bother you but still you can leave whenever you wish. You know that when you do leave, you can always come back.

6. You might enjoy one of these places:

    a. Make yourself comfortable and close your eyes. Then sit on the bank of a rippling stream, cool water trickling over moss-covered rocks and old tree limbs.

Above you leafy branches form a cave over your head and across to the other side. Take off your shoes and put your feet into the water. Wiggle your toes in the fine silt that rests on the bottom. Lean back against the rough bark of a maple and watch the water swirl into foam. When you are completely relaxed, allow your imagination to bring you back where you started.

b. Close your eyes and imagine that you are a bird, a crow maybe, free-soaring and boundless, able to fly on forever.

17

Lift into the air, talons tucked back against your body, feathers sleek in the wind. You fly over fields of tawny wheat just after a rain, smelling the freshness of the loamy earth. Next you soar and spiral above a vast, wide river, water smashing and roiling over rocks and falls.

You decide to follow the river to its source atop a snow-covered mountain.

You pause to hear the sound of crashing water, the cry of other birds. Feel the air caressing your wings and back. Soar on and on and on, then settle gently to earth and back to the place you started.

c. Close your eyes and imagine yourself in a cabin up in the mountains. Outside the snow is falling in fluffy white flakes, covering earth and trees and rocks in a blanket as soft as feathers. Through the window you see it is getting on toward evening, the sun just above the giant pine trees on a distant hill, illuminating the earth like the flame from a giant candle.

You light a roaring blaze in the fireplace, then sit in the middle of a large braided rug, your legs drawn up, encircled by your arms, chin resting on your knees. The fire is hot on your face as you watch the flames flicker blue and white and red. In these flames you see the scene of your happiest memories. Take time now to watch the scenes unfold and regain those feelings of happiness. When you're ready, transport yourself back to where you started and open your eyes.

7. For this exercise you will be a little more on your own; you'll need to use your imagination a little more than for the other exercises. This one will take you to the most beautiful place you have ever seen. But it's only yours. Once you are there, you should take time to make it what you want it to be, to explore it so that it relaxes you completely and fills you with peace and serenity. You'll be there alone, to enjoy it by yourself. Later, if you like, you can lead your classmates there on a fantasy trip, but it's not necessary. Here is how you get there:

Imagine a frozen pond on the edge of a town when the air is as cold as crystal, and you can see off to the furthest star.

You put on a pair of magic skates that make you better than

Hans Brinker or an Olympic champion. Stand then and skate toward the end of the pond miles and miles distant. You begin to pick up speed, faster and faster, flashing past trees and people on the shore and houses and barns and towns, faster and faster and faster. Everything becomes a blur, and you're skating so fast that you've come to the furthest reaches of time and the universe. Gradually, you slow and finally stop in the most beautiful spot you've ever imagined, entirely different from the world you've always known. Take off your skates and spend as long as you like exploring, enjoying everything you see. You're free to make it what you wish — to walk or sit or fly from corner to corner, east to west, north to south. Gather up the peacefulness and the beauty so you can take it back with you.

Anytime you wish, just blink, and you will be back in your classroom.

At the end of two or three minutes your teacher will gently call everyone back. If you open your eyes before the time is up, sit quietly until everyone else has returned.

SLOW AND EASY

The following two exercises start you off slow and easy and help you become accustomed to performing in front of others.

1. Write down on a piece of paper a simple activity that you perform everyday. It can be something like: a) brushing my hair; b) getting a snack after school; c) playing a tape or CD. Now trade papers with someone else. Using the activity written on the paper you received, present a 30- to 60-second pantomime. Have the class try to figure out what it is you're doing.

2. Write on a piece of paper an activity that some people do everyday, but not you. It can be something like: a) a bank teller cashing a check for a customer; b) a veterinarian giving a cat or dog an injection; c) a carpenter building a cabinet. Trade papers with someone else. Use the activity on the paper you received to present a 30- to 60-second pantomime showing the activity.

3. This is similar to the last two exercises. Write down an activity that is unusual 1) in that most people do it but only rarely, 2) or else few people do it at all. An example of the former is winning a big award at school and of the latter, feeding the animals at the zoo.

4. You can have a day or two to think about this activity. It should be something that's done by a character from legend or from a well-known story. Write the activity and the character on paper and then trade with someone. Perform a 30- to 60-second pantomime. Have the class guess who you were and what you were doing. Examples might be Jack or Jill going up the hill with a pail for water, or Androcles pulling a thorn from the lion's foot.

JUST FOR FUN

These exercises are a little different but don't take a lot of planning, so you should relax and have fun with them.

1. Show that you are either too hot or too cold, but try to do it in a way that's different from what people usually do.

2. Along with a partner create and describe a whole new world or universe, maybe similar to the one to which you skated.

Take two or three days to work out a fantasy trip there. Then have your classmates lean back in their chairs, or, if possible, lie on the floor, eyes closed, and take them on a guided tour in a way that is similar to the other fantasy trips all of you have already taken. You may talk from notes or an outline, or write out the whole thing.

If you wish, you can use the place you visited in Exercise 6.

3. Get together with a partner. One of you should be Little Red Riding Hood and the other one of the Three Little Pigs. Hold a 30- to 60-second discussion of your views on wolves. Maybe it will help if you start by asking each other's opinions.

4. Choose a historical figure, such as Harry Truman or Joan of Arc. Get together with a partner who has chosen a different historical figure. Pretend you meet on the city bus or at the library. Now take a minute or so to explain something from your own time period to the other person, which would be outside the character's realm of experience. An example might be Thomas Edison trying to explain the light bulb to Michelangelo. Or Nero explaining the Roman games to Eric the Red.

5. Your teacher will play instrumental music. Each of you should listen until you feel or think of a mood the music evokes. Now go to the playing area in front of the class and move in rhythm to the music but trying to portray the mood you feel. Don't use the usual dance steps you know. Rather try to be completely expressive of the mood.

6. Visualize a blank piece of paper. Now visualize first one word on the paper, then two words and then a phrase or a sentence. Think of a person or a character who might logically say what you have "written" on the page in your mind. Tell the class the words and the character you think would say them.

7. Spend an hour or two as if you possessed a certain physical trait you do not possess. For instance, if you're tall, pretend you're short. Then tell the rest of the class how this made you feel.

8. Spend an hour or two as if you possessed a personality trait you don't possess. For instance, if you're outgoing, pretend you're shy, or vice versa. Take a few moments to tell the class how this made you view the world and think differently.

9. In front of the class communicate a mood or an emotion through:

a. gestures, posture and stance;

b. gestures alone;

c. posture alone.

10. Think of a historical character and the period in which he or she lived. Imagine that you can travel back and talk to that person. However, you can tell him only two things that will change history for the better. Remember the person knows nothing about our time. So what will you say that convinces him or her to try to change the way things are? You can have a couple of days to think about this. When you're ready, set up two chairs in the playing area. You take one and imagine the historical figure in the other. Let the class eavesdrop on what you say.

11. Imagine yourself in this picture.

Answer these things about yourself:

a. What are you doing here?

b. Where are you from?

c. Are you enjoying the day? Why?

d. What is your life like, generally?

Share your life with the class. You can have three or four days to plan this out. Then play one of the characters in the picture giving a monolog that lasts about two minutes.

12. That is a game called "Here's what we did when . . ." The idea is that you start with this phrase and then add something

silly to it. Then everyone has to come up with an answer. If you can't think of anything right away, it's okay to pass once in a while. Try to make your answers as silly as the problem. Here are a few to start you off.

Here's what we did when:

a. we discovered the boy next door was a mummy;

b. all those fish invaded our living room;

c. we started getting calls from the Martians;

d. dinosaurs started hatching from all those eggs we bought;

e. the wild hamsters surrounded our house.

After everyone has responded to each of these, come up with situations of your own.

Don't worry about how "dumb" your answer is. The idea is always to let yourself go and not worry about how things sound.

Remember you're not to be judgmental, nor to make fun of anyone for what they do. The idea is that you should let your imagination soar.

13. You are the only one in the world who knows the person in this picture. To establish his identity, take 60 seconds to tell the class who he is and how you happen to know him.

14. This is called, "Oh, How I Tried." You begin by saying, "I was trying to [whatever it is] but _____." Fill in the blank by telling what happened as a result.

Figure out answers to these and then come up with some of your own. Go around the room with each person answering each problem in a different way.

I was trying to:

a. fill the pool with Jello, but —

b. harness the turtles to take me to town, but —

c. have tea with the giant amoebas, but —

d. make an ice cream cone as tall as Mount Everest, but —

e. saddle my unicorn, but —

15. Choose a partner and begin at opposite ends of the playing space. When you reach the center, greet each other without using words, but in one of the following ways:

a. as jealous siblings;

b. as a husband and wife who have just gotten a divorce;

c. as long-lost friends;

d. as two muggers looking for victims;

e. as two rivals for the same boyfriend/girlfriend;

f. as two plainclothesmen, who don't know each other and are looking for a robbery suspect;

g. as two neighbors who dislike each other;

h. as two athletes from rival teams a day after the big game;

i. as a movie star and an ardent fan;

j. as a lawyer and a client whose case he lost;

k. as a playwright and the critic who panned his play.

Don't tell the class ahead of time which one you will do. Have them try to figure it out afterward.

16. Somehow a whale has been stranded far from the ocean.

Get together in groups of four or five and figure out a way to get him back to the ocean. You can have five minutes to come up with a plan. Then a spokesman from each group will tell the rest of the class how his or her group thinks the job can best be done. After all the groups have reported, the class will discuss the merits of each plan. Afterwards the groups will meet again to take into consideration what was said in the discussion. You can use any suggestions you think were good. Each group should then present a two- to three-minute pantomime showing how you are taking the whale back to the ocean.

17. Place yourself in this picture.

Look around once you are there. Where is this place? How did you get there? Do you like it? How does it make you feel? What would you like to do there? How long would you like to stay? Think about these things and jot down notes if you like. Then tell the class all about your experiences there. Answer all the questions about the place and any others that you think of that might help tell anything about it. You can have five minutes to think about what to say. Then your teacher will have each of you tell the rest of the class all about your journey there. Each telling should take a minute to 90 seconds.

18. Each of you will get your chance to play the advice columnist, "Dear Blabby." To provide questions, each of you should come up with problems that need to be solved. They shouldn't be real problems, but rather should be either funny or bizarre. For example, "My pet rabbit thinks he's a dog. He barks and chases my cat up trees. What can I do to show him he's wrong?"

You have till the next class meeting to come up with four questions, which you should write on separate slips of paper. Your teacher will collect these and place them in a container at the beginning of the class.

One by one each of you will go to the front of the room and sit in a chair. The teacher will allow you to pick out three questions, one at a time. After reading each question, you can ad-lib an answer. Try to make the answer as offbeat and humorous as possible.

Part II:

ACTING GAMES

Learning to Be Sensitive

Many go through life paying little attention to the things or the people around them, even to their own feelings. To do a good job on stage, you have to be able to *feel* both physically and emotionally.

For example, when you eat a piece of fresh fruit, you need to be aware of the shape and texture, the odor and the taste.

You have to be in touch with your own feelings. This means "getting inside" yourself and understanding exactly how you feel at any moment and why you feel that way. Then you need to bring this new understanding to each role that you play. Finally, as a character in an improvisation or a play, you have to be sensitive to how others feel.

To do these things, you need to learn to pay attention, to be in touch with the world, yourself and others.

BEING IN TOUCH WITH THE WORLD AROUND YOU

1. Here's something you can do on your own. Pretend you'll be leaving tomorrow on a spaceship that will head out to distant galaxies. Because of the way space time works, you'll age more slowly on your flight than will the people back on Earth. You know this; you know that when you return, you'll be middle-aged. Your friends' children's children will be the same age as you.

Going on this journey is an honor for you and your family; it's an opportunity few have. Yet you'll be giving up everyone and everything you hold dear.

So when you go home this afternoon, look at each room, each piece of furniture, each picture on the wall with the knowledge that you'll never see them again. Because of this, you'll want to memorize all their details, to hold them in your mind.

As you visit each room and closely examine it, think what memories each object calls up. What does each mean to you? What part has it played in your life? Think about all the people who sat in the easy chair, who watched television or listened to music.

These are all emotional memories, but now think about physical sensations as well. Run your hand over the back of the sofa or

31

the arm of the chair. How does it feel to your touch?

What are the special odors of your house? The smell of coffee always ready for pouring? The soft scents of perfume, your father's shaving lotion? If you stop and listen, what sounds do you hear — traffic, animals, kids playing outside, a radio off in the distance.

What foods have you tasted here and enjoyed that you'll never again taste because the person who cooked them will no longer be there when you return?

The most difficult thing is that this is your last chance to see those people who are important to you, your family and friends and relatives.

Memorize the clothes they wear, what they say, the special sounds of their voices. Look closely into their faces. What do you see? How do you feel about each of them? How does each feel about you? Think about these things and imprint them forever on your brain.

Of course, this is only an exercise, and you'll see all these things and these people again and again. But don't let the familiarity of it all deaden your senses.

To help you become more aware, you need to develop your *sense memory*. That means remembering how things feel or sound, how they taste and smell, how they look and what it's like to feel movement and heat or cold.

To develop sense memory, just as you did in Exercise 1, pay attention to the ordinary, to everything around you. The following exercises will help you with this.

2. The next time you eat an apple, feel how heavy it is in your hand. Feel the texture of the skin. See that it has different shades of red in various streaks, that parts of it are yellow or green. Inhale its odor both before and after you've taken that first bite. Feel the apple skin on your tongue, the whiteness and juiciness inside. Do this with whatever you taste or see or hear.

    a. Eat an orange, experiencing the same things as you did with the apple. Feel the differences among the textures of the skin, the outside of each section, and the inside.

    b. Stand outside in a gentle rain. How does it feel against your face? What are the special smells of the earth in this rain? Think about how the grass looks glazed with water. Pay attention to the beads of rain on cars and the sides of houses.

c. Feel the spray of water against your body in the shower, the sight of the steam, the smell of the soap and shampoo, the squeaky clean feel of your hair.

d. Feel and smell the fresh clothes that you put on each morning. Feel the weight of the shirt or top against your back and arms, the texture of the clothing, its temperature.

You can build your sense memories with everything you do.

3. In front of the class pantomime eating an orange or apple, or drinking a soda, a glass of water or a cup of coffee or tea. Choose whatever you like, but be prepared. Know, for example, exactly how much space a plum takes and exactly what is involved in eating it. Remember this and portray it exactly. Choose to evoke whatever sense memory you like, but make the rest of the class really see the invisible object in your hand.

4. Your teacher will bring a number of objects like ceramic pots, tools or other household objects to the classroom and place them in various locations. Team up with someone else, who will lead you around the room to feel the objects and identify them just by touch. You're to be blindfolded or to keep your eyes closed. Even if it's easy to tell what the object is, really concentrate on feeling its varying textures, its shape, and how heavy it is. Also feel larger objects like desks and doorways and molding. At the end of five minutes switch places with your partner.

When you've finished, ask yourself what you observed that was not apparent to you before this.

GETTING IN TOUCH WITH YOURSELF

5. For this exercise, sit comfortably in a chair or on the floor. Then think about the different sensations you feel physically. How do your shoes fit your feet? What does the collar feel like around your neck? The belt or elastic around your waist? The fabric against your thighs and legs? Is anything too tight? Too loose? If you're wearing any jewelry, feel it against your skin. How do the various pieces of clothing feel different from each other?

Now concentrate on aches and pains, on undue pressures that make you even a little uncomfortable, on any places that you itch.

If you concentrate like this, you'll feel a lot of things that you're not normally aware of and which most of the time you can block out but can recall when you need to use them for portraying a character or a scene or in empathizing or understanding how another character feels.

6. Your teacher will time two minutes when you simply sit quietly trying to hear as many different sounds as you can — in the room, in the hallway and outside. You should be able to hear at least a dozen different sounds and maybe a lot more.

When the time is up, write down all of those you remember. As a class, begin listing them. Were there any that your classmates heard that you didn't? Who heard the most?

All of these things are important because they help you more accurately portray feelings. They help assure that you'll be convincing in the things you do in front of an audience.

7. Get into the habit of analyzing why you feel each emotion you do. Why do you react a certain way? Psychologists often say that other people don't make you feel things. You're responsible for the way you feel in relation to events or other people. It's not that your siblings make you angry. You make yourself angry in reaction to them. Often something that causes one person to feel angry will simply make another person laugh. What is unique about you and your emotions? Why do you react in certain ways?

8. Take a few moments to look at each of the photos on page 35. Then write down what emotions each makes you feel. Why do you think you feel this way?

Discuss your feelings with the class and see if others felt differently. If so, why did they? If you want to, you can explain why you think each photo made you feel as it did.

There's a technique that actors sometimes use called *emotional memory*. For most performances you don't need to use it. It's a last resort if you're having trouble feeling a particular emotion in improvising a scene or performing a role in a play. To use emotional memory, remember when you felt the emotion you want to portray for the audience.

Suppose, for instance, that you want to do a scene in which you're happy. Most often you just need to think of the situation that you're to portray, and you can feel the emotion. You identify or empathize with the character.

But if you're having trouble with this, you can use emotional memory. The idea behind it is that it's impossible to recall just an emotion. Instead, you recall the circumstances. Remember exactly where you were, who you were with, and everything that happened, and soon you'll feel the happiness.

Another technique is to assume the facial expression and the posture of a particular emotion. For instance, let your shoulders sag, pull down the corners of your mouth, and squint a little bit, and you may start to feel sad.

If you smile and keep on smiling, chances are you're going to get into a better mood.

9. Use emotional memory of facial expression to make yourself feel:

a. fear

b. happiness

c. anger

d. disgust

e. sadness

f. surprise

g. resentment

h. anxiety

i. frustration

j. loneliness

10. Inside this store (shown on page 37) you can find anything you need to dress up as a particular character or for a particular occasion.

You need choose only a few items of clothing, such as a top hat, cane and tails. Then present a pantomime in which you don the clothes, pick up the prop and use it. You can present this exercise as yourself or as a character. Each pantomime should be about two minutes long.

11. Figure out what emotions the characters are feeling in the following scenes. Choose one excerpt and with a partner read the lines in front of the class.

When you finish, ask yourself if you felt the emotion. If not, try again. When you do feel it, tell the rest of the class what the emotion was and which technique you think you used to feel it — empathy, emotional memory, or assuming the facial expression.

In this scene from "Going Steady," Martin allowed Karen to "see" a watch that has been passed down for several generations in his family. She manages to get it away from him without giving it back. This occurs the next day at school.

MARTIN: I want my watch back, Karen.
KAREN: I don't have it.

MARTIN: What?!

KAREN: I gave it to Millie to look at.

MARTIN: You had no right to do that.

KAREN: You'll get your precious watch back.

MARTIN: Well, I'd better.

> *(KAREN turns away.)*
>
> **Karen!**
>
> *(KAREN turns back.)*
>
> Why did you tell the other kids we're going together?

KAREN: It's none of your business.

MARTIN: I want you to tell them it isn't true.

KAREN: Tell them yourself.

MARTIN: *(As KAREN turns to leave, he grabs her arm and spins her around.)* You'd better tell them today, and you'd better give my watch back!

This is an excerpt from "Are You Happy?"

MAN: I'm taking a poll, you know like the Gallup Poll, only a little different.

WOMAN: I suppose you're going to ask me something dumb like "Why?" Why do I exist? Why does the world exist? Why is humankind made to suffer?

MAN: Quite the contrary. I just want to know: Are you happy?

WOMAN: *(Begins to laugh softly and the laughter builds till she becomes hysterical with it as she tries to answer.)* Am — I — hap — py? Oh, my goodness. Happy. *(Suddenly serious)* What the hell is happy?! Nobody in her right mind's happy. Is that it? You think I'm crazy. Well, let me tell you something, damn it. *(Begins shouting.)* Sane. Do you understand me, I'm sane. I've had enough of your silliness. I don't know what you're trying to pull anyhow.

MAN: *(Indignant)* I'm not trying to pull anything. It's a simple question that requires a simple answer. Are

you happy?

WOMAN: **How dare you insult me like this? How dare you?**

MAN: **I'm sorry if you think I've been insulting. I didn't
mean to be insulting. I was out of work. The economy. I used to own my own business, a nice retail
establishment. But the economy. Then I found this
job, and I was happy.**

12. Think of an emotion such as disgust. Think of a reason
for someone's being disgusted. Now create a character who is
disgusted for this reason. What does the person say and do? To
whom is he or she speaking? Where are they? Describe the environment and the circumstances. Write all this down and share it
with the class. Now try the same thing with other emotions such
as anger or jealousy.

GETTING IN TOUCH WITH OTHERS

Try to see what makes each person unique, how he or she
differs from anyone else. How does one of your friends react to a
joke as compared to another? How does one person's sneeze differ

from another's? The following exercises are to help you become more aware of other people.

13. When you go to a store the next time, observe and listen to what other people say. If possible, watch a particular person for a minute or two. Watch his or her actions and listen to the dialog. What is the tone of voice? What do you think the person's mood is? What do you base that on? Pay attention to traits and habits. How does the person move?

Write a character sketch a page or so long stating everything you know and can guess about the person. Read this to the rest of the class, who can then ask you questions about the one you observed.

14. Go to a store or mall. Try to discover three distinctive traits about someone there, things that make him or her different from most other people. Maybe the person frowns constantly or has a nervous habit, such as constantly pushing glasses up over the nose. Do this with three different people. Then present a pantomime in front of the class where you pretend to be one of the people you observed. Include the three unusual traits along with the usual ones. See if the rest of the class can pick them out and if they think the traits are unusual.

15. Look at this photo.

Discuss with the class:

a. The things you can tell for certain about the people in the photo.

b. The things you can guess about them.

c. How do others in the class see them differently? Why do you think this is so? Who do you think is right and why?

16. Be a people watcher. Begin keeping a file of "characters." Observe how people move, talk, respond, eat or drink, or express strong emotions. When you see anything unusual, write it down. This can help you in playing a particular type of person or in acting in a convincing manner.

17. What makes your favorite relative special to you? What traits of this person's do you most admire? Why? Write a paragraph or two about this and read it to the class. Unless you want to, you don't have to list the person's name.

18. Sometimes we expect people who dress or wear their hair a certain way to have a particular type of personality. For instance, we expect women with bleached hair, dangling earrings and lots of bracelets to be loud or outgoing.

Look at these photos and determine what you think each would be like if you could meet them in person.

41

19. Go to a store or shopping mall and pick out someone you expect to be a certain way. Base this on your first impression, and jot the reaction down in a notebook or tablet. Watch the person gesture and move. Now go closer and hear what he or she says. Were there any surprises?

Do this with two or three more people. What about them was as you expected it to be? What was different? Now figure out what made you think of them in the way that you did. Share with the class what you discovered.

Exercises such as this and the one that follows help you see people as individuals, even though they may look similar, and to tear down stereotypes.

20. Take one of the people you've observed, and in front of the class, walk across the room as this person would walk, using the same mannerisms. Then talk about the weather or a movie you're going to see, but do this the way the person you watched would do it.

21. Listen to a short conversation — 30 seconds or so — at school, at home or at a store. Now write down as much of it as you can remember. Exchange papers with someone else. Read to the class what the other person has written, and have the class try to figure out the mood of each of the speakers.

22. From observing others, you can tell that each person has many unique qualities. Even people who have similar jobs or grew up in similar areas are different from each other. When you do the following think of a specific person, whether or not he or she actually fits the type of situation or job. Then go off stage or to the side of the playing area and enter the stage or space, pantomiming:

a. A police officer who has come to tell a mother that her 15-year-old was in a serious accident;

b. A teenager who has just failed a driver's exam and has to tell a friend;

c. An obstetrician who comes to tell a young man his wife has had a baby girl;

d. A department store clerk coming home from work the day after Christmas, usually the busiest day of the year;

e. A teenager who has just been fired from a first job and has to tell a parent;

f. A young married person having to tell a spouse that the promotion at work did not come through;

g. A first-time actor who has flubbed a big speech;

h. A speaker who is half an hour late for a talk;

i. A high school student coming home after being told of winning a full-tuition scholarship;

j. A supervisor having to fire a person who desperately needs money;

k. A football player entering the locker room after missing a field goal that cost his team the championship;

l. A woman swimmer coming home after setting a world record for her event;

m. A scientist entering the auditorium to receive the Nobel Prize for finding a cure for a serious illness;

n. A newspaper reporter getting to the political rally just as it ends;

o. A clergyman who is late for the wedding;

p. A musician coming up on stage to accept an Oscar for his song.

Freeing the Imagination

All the exercises in this section involve breaking old thinking patterns so you can more easily open up your mind to new approaches. Maybe Point A to Point B is the shortest route, but it might be more fun and so more productive to go from Point A to Point X to Point B.

This is what acting or any other form of creativity is all about, breaking rules, expanding the boundaries. Often, those who go the furthest in developing something new are the ones who are considered the best at what they do.

In the sensitivity training activities, you saw that you can expand your thinking or awareness to include many new things. In this section you see that you can go even further. You can develop whole new ways of thinking by going outside the lines as the artist did in this drawing.

Although the wing and beak of one bird and the wing tip of another are the only things outside the boundaries, still there's a feeling of freedom, of escape. This makes the drawing more alive; it gives it more a sense of freedom and abandon than if the two birds were entirely inside the frame.

The artist broke the usual rules; she became an innovator of sorts, giving her viewers a drawing that was more fun to see.

No doubt she first learned to stay within the frame of the picture. Only later did she probably tell herself that it was okay to do things a little differently.

By expanding your view of the world, you have much more to draw on for improvisations or acting.

1. Here are two drawings.

They're somewhat abstract; yet it's easy to tell they represent men. The first has parts missing; the second is made up of lines and a dot. The drawings break the rules and yet convey the idea that these are men. Why do you suppose they were drawn this way? What do the drawings tell you about the way the artist viewed the world? What is she saying about the two men? What sort of men are they?

Choose one of the two drawings. Write down on a slip of paper one or two words that describe either of the two men. Now go in front of the class and by facial expression and stance convey what you know or surmised about the one you chose. Have the class try to figure out what it is. If they do guess correctly, let them know. If they don't, read what you've written on the paper. After several people have been in front of the class, talk about all of your reasons for drawing the conclusions you did about the two men.

2. What do you think would be a good title for this picture? Tell the rest of the class why you think so.

The next three exercises are just plain silly and probably are different from anything you've done before. They are 1) to "bend" your mind and so change the way you think and 2) to show you that it's perfectly all right to do something that appears to have no goal.

3. Before school, pick up a pebble and spend a few moments examining it. Note its color and feeling, its weight and its texture and shape. Carry it with you all day and all evening. Place it by your bed for the night. When you're getting ready for school the next day, put the pebble in your pocket or purse. Then some time before school starts, take it out and place it on the ground and never look at it again.

If you wish, you can tell the class about it or do a pantomime showing how you found it, took it home and placed it by your bed and then how you placed it on the ground. But you don't have to do that unless you want to.

4. Ask your mom or dad or another adult for an object the person no longer wants. Take the object to class and trade with the first person you see. It doesn't matter if the person has already traded with someone else. Now you can either keep the new object or throw it away. If you decide to keep it, spend a couple of minutes writing a letter to yourself telling why you want it. If you decide to throw it away, spend a couple of minutes writing a letter to yourself telling why you did not want it. Fold the letter into the tiniest square you can and carry it home and throw it into the trash. Or if you like, you can ask a relative or friend to put it away for the next five and a half weeks and then throw it away.

5. The next time you're out walking find a leaf near a tree. Pick it up and place it under a different tree. But you must make sure there's a leaf there already so you can pick it up. Do this three more times. If anyone asks what you're doing, tell them the story of Little Red Riding Hood or ignore them completely. Toss the last leaf over your shoulder and don't look back.

Write a silly poem about how this exercise made you feel, but don't ever show it to anyone. You can get up in front and *recite* it to your classmates if you like. Or else hide it in a drawer and don't look at it again until next January 1.

The next few exercises are to show you different ways for you to be as creative as you want to be while still following directions.

6. Decide what animal you would choose to become if you could not be a human being. Take a few moments to think about that animal and to see it in your mind. Pay attention to how it walks and moves and the way it carries itself. Then stand and begin circling the room slowly, gradually transforming yourself into that animal. You can use posture, walk, carriage and body gestures to show what animal you are. Once the transformation is complete, face your classmates and gradually become yourself once more.

7. Bring paints or crayons and paper to class. Your teacher will play a record. As you listen to the record, paint or color a picture

47

of how the music makes you feel. Match the lines and forms to the rhythm and melody, the color to the changing moods. Don't even think about how the picture looks, whether it's "good" or not. That doesn't matter. All that does matter is that you capture your thoughts and feelings about what you hear.

Now take two or three minutes to think about your picture and what it means to you — without really trying to describe how it looks on the paper. Write a paragraph or two explaining this. Your teacher will collect the paragraphs and place them in a hat or box and then collect the pictures, number them and arrange them in rows on the floor.

Each of you will draw a paper from the hat or box and read what it says to the rest of the class, who will try to match each paragraph to each picture. The person who has the most correct answers wins a yellow star! (At the back of the book are models for stars; your teacher will tell you how they are to be used.)

8. Imagine yourself in this picture.

Imagine yourself going into this house back in 1905 when this picture was taken. Imagine what you see there — the furniture, the furnishings, the people. How are you related to these people? Are you a friend, a next door neighbor? How many people are in the house? What about the one who is missing? Where is he and what does the government have to do with it? Has he truly done anything wrong? How do the others in the room feel about what he has done? How do you feel? What are you going to do about it? How does this make you want to treat the people in the house? How will they react?

This is your most complex exercise so far. Get into groups of four, two girls and two boys in each group. Next, each person in each group should think individually about the questions and take three or four days to write a story about what happened in connection with the house. Then in class each person will tell the rest of the group his or her story. Then you are to present a scene based on each of the stories, with the members of the group playing the roles.

Do just one story and scene per day in each group. Don't write the dialog out but improvise based on the story. Do try to portray the character as the writer visualized him or her. Each scene should be at least three minutes but no longer than five.

9. Now place yourself in this setting.

All of these people have something to do with this house. Are they related by blood, or tied together in some other way?

The last exercise asked questions you had to answer. This time you have to think up the questions as well. Keep the same groups you had in the last exercise. But this time you are to work together in coming up with only one story. Take at least two or three class periods to work together to create it. Again, don't bother to write it out in dialog, but improvise a four-minute scene based on it. Present the scene for the rest of the class.

10. Your teacher has slips of paper in a hat or box. On each slip of paper is a color. Draw one of the slips and read the name of the color; visualize how it looks. Then think of how it makes you feel. As your teacher calls on you, go to the front of the room and present a pantomime showing this. You can make the movements either specific or symbolic. For example, suppose you drew the color red, and you decide it makes you feel too warm. You can pantomime fanning yourself and so on. Or if you draw blue, you can move in a rhythm that suggests sadness, such as closing your eyes, tightening your lips and throwing back your head.

Have the class try to guess the color. If the first person to answer has correctly figured out your color, your teacher will give you a yellow star!

11. The sign on the door reads only "The Escape." But those seeking the sort of adventure most people have never dreamed of are often told that this is the place to find it.

Walk into the building, into a vast empty space and shake hands with the General who comes to greet you. "If you agree to the price," he tells you, "you can be assured of the greatest adventure . . ."

You know you've come to the right spot. But where does it lead? You are the only one who knows because it's your adventure and yours alone. Whom do you meet there? What happens?

You have a week to write up your adventure. Then take five minutes to tell the class about your experience beyond "The Escape." Make this a combination of telling and pantomime. For example, if you went on a safari, show how you stalked a dangerous leopard and what happened when the two of you came face to face.

12. A good way of learning to look at the world differently is

to spend time as someone else. So for an hour or two look at the world as if you were one of these:

a. Your favorite teacher ever;

b. Your grandmother or grandfather;

c. A two-year-old child;

d. The person you most dislike in the whole world;

e. Your brother, sister or cousin;

f. A person you've observed and listened to in a mall or store;

g. Another person whom you choose.

Spend your hour or two living as that person. See others as this person does. View the world as he or she does. Is there anything different now about your outlook on life? How do you feel about your home or neighborhood, the school, the city in which you live? How do you feel about the person that used to be you before you became someone else?

Write a page or more telling what you learned about this person that you became.

Present a 30-second pantomime showing how the one you became appears and moves. Try to use a particular habit or gesture or way of walking he or she has.

After you've finished, tell the class about the person. Explain your choice, how you felt seeing the world as he or she did, and if your feelings about the person have changed in any way.

Any time in your life that you feel you don't understand someone or you disagree with something that is done or said, it might help to try living for a time and viewing life as that person. There's an old saying that contains a lot of truth. "Don't criticize someone until you've walked in his moccasins."

13. You have just come upon one of the largest outdoor stages in the country. You're with a wealthy companion who tells you he will rent the space and invite everyone in the city to come watch you perform. Besides that, he will pay you the fantastic salary of five million dollars if you can but hold your audience enthralled. The performance — a pantomime of exquisite artistry — must last for at least 60 seconds. In one week's time, you'll be called upon to do your stuff, and the world will see if your friend's

51

faith in you was justified.

14. What type of person is this?

Speak as she would for 30 seconds to a minute on one of the following:

a. Today's teenagers;

b. What is wrong with this country;

c. The importance of culture in our lives;

d. My type of friend;

e. How I spent my last vacation, and how you should spend yours;

f. The role of television in contemporary society.

15. Talk for a minute on one of the topics that follows, but portray an emotion different from the one usually associated with that topic. For example, show fright when you talk about brushing your teeth.

a. Taking an exam;

b. Winning a prize;

c. Falling and breaking an arm;

d. Watching my favorite TV show;

e. Brushing my hair;

f. Getting caught in the rain;

g. Getting to school late;

h. Playing a game of checkers;

i. Cutting my fingernails;

j. Eating dinner.

16. A tall tale is a story that is filled with exaggeration, including things that could not really happen and characters that simply could not be true. This exercise begins with the words, "Tell me about the time you . . ." The way this works is that each of you should write two different ideas such as "fell off the cliff," "captured the giant mongoose in the waters off the Alaskan coast," "made pets of the saber-toothed tigers."

Your teacher will collect your ideas, look over them, discard duplicates or any phrases that he or she thinks are inappropriate. The following day each of you will draw one of these slips from a box. You'll have three or four minutes to think up a tall tale about the topic you drew. Then you'll go to the front and tell the story to the class. Exaggerate and make the stories as outrageous as you can.

17. Think of a fairy tale. When the teacher calls on you, get up in front of the class and tell the story. The catch is that you can't use real language but only gibberish. However, you can use pantomime to make your story as convincing as possible. For example, you can show Goldilocks trying each chair until she finds the one that's right and so on. When you finish, the others in the class will tell you what story they think you told. If the first answer is correct, you'll receive a yellow star.

18. Here's a list of characters: William Shakespeare, the U.S. President, John Wilkes Booth, Picasso, Ringo Starr, Pinocchio, Romeo, Dear Abby, Martha Washington and Dolly Parton. Your teacher will ask you to come up with more names, so you end up with as many as there are members in your class. Put the names of males in one container, females in another. Each of you will draw a slip of paper with one of the names. You'll have 20

seconds to go in front of the class as the character whose name you drew and say:

I know I'm going to be in a very bad accident. Before it happens time will stop, and here's what I'm going to do:

The only thing you can't do is interfere with the crash or stop its happening. Your answers can be either funny or serious, but they have to be something that would be logical for the character to know about and want to do.

19. It is believed that theatre of a sort began in primitive times when people sat around a campfire enacting events that had occurred. Gradually, or so the theory goes, these reenactments became a kind of ritual to please the gods. Here's a list of things that primitive people may have reenacted.

a. The hunt

b. Moving to a new location

c. The harvest

d. Building a dwelling

e. A worship ritual to please the gods

Get into groups of four to six people and choose one of these things and plan out a pantomime. Try to get together to rehearse a few times before you present it. Take a week to plan it out. You can use hand props if you wish, but it's not necessary.

20. Think of what might have been other important events in the lives of prehistoric people. Go to the front of the class and begin pantomiming one of these things. As soon as your classmates understand what you're doing, they can come up front and continue the activity with you. You can use nonverbal sounds but not real words. Be as expressive as you can with these sounds.

21. Choose one of the following sentences. Then plan out a 20- to 30-second pantomime that illustrates it. You have two or three minutes to plan it out. Then have the rest of the class figure out which sentence you're illustrating. For instance, you could pantomime the first sentence by looking through an imaginary purse or wallet, or by turning your pockets inside out.

a. I wish I could afford it.

b. In my day, people had a little respect for each other.

54

c. I've never felt like this before in my life.

d. Why do these things always happen to me?

e. I wish he hadn't done that.

f. This is the most incredible day of my life.

g. I hate it when everything goes wrong.

h. What's the matter with you, huh?

i. There's got to be a better way to do this.

j. I've always wanted to have this experience.

If the first answer you receive is correct, you'll get a yellow star!

22. One of you should start by saying: My friend is just like a _____ because . . . In the blank space use the name of an object in describing an imaginary friend. For instance:

My friend is just like an *elephant* because:

• Elephants trumpet and so does he.

• He remembers everything.

• Her skin is so grey-looking.

• He has such big feet.

• Her nose is so big.

Go around the room until nobody can think of anything else that fits.

Here is a list of objects to use: *rag doll, old car, egg, horse, cheetah, hurricane, shooting star, rhinoceros, rock, ocean wave, tree, baby.* You can come up with more words if you like.

23. Someone should write each of these adjectives and nouns on different slips of paper: *cold, blue, rainy, stupendous, colorful, tiny, rocky, soft, healthy, shifty, big, slippery, stern, brown, hardy, humorous, gentle, aged, lacy, fanciful, red, fluffy, bright, ignorant, trembling* and *bird, person, stone, cheese, heaven, dog, castle, mouth, kitten, clock, ball, train, mountain, child, hand, head, cup, light, stars, beach, suitcase, room, maid, lawn, woman.* Put all 50 slips in a box or hat. Each person should draw two words. It doesn't matter whether you get an adjective and a noun. Two of either is just as good. Once you've drawn the words, you're to write a story in which you logically use both words but *not* at the same

55

time, like *fluffy bird*. The words have to be separated by at least two sentences. For instance:

One day there was an old man walking along the street, and he spied a wedge of *cheese* lying on a piece of paper on the sidewalk. He was very hungry, so he grabbed the cheese and ran.

"Hey, mister," a little boy called, "you don't have to run away. It's my cheese, and I'll be glad to share it with you."

The man heard him and returned. When he looked closely, he saw that the boy looked familiar. "Is your name Donald?" the old man asked. The boy looked like the old man's little son who'd been kidnapped by a cheesemaker years earlier.

"No," said the boy. "But a bad man who makes cheese kidnapped me way across the sea and brought me here. I stole this big piece of cheese and ran away."

"Why was it lying on the sidewalk?" the old man said.

"It's magic cheese," the boy said. "When you give it away, you gain much more than you've given. I wanted to be sure someone saw it."

"Are you certain?" the old man asked.

"Of course," said the boy.

"Then I accept." The old man broke off a piece of cheese and handed it to the boy. Then he broke off a piece for himself. Suddenly, the cheese turned to gold.

"Gracious me," said the old man, "now we can buy food so neither of us has to be hungry."

"And I can get back across the sea to find my mother."

"And I shall find my son."

They immediately booked passage on a great ship and sailed off together. After arriving in port, they continued on till the boy found his mother, which made the old man happy. It also made him sad.

After giving half the gold to the boy, the old man went off by himself. Little did he know that the next ticket he bought would be punched by the conductor of a mighty iron horse, and the conductor would be his long lost son Donald. For years the boy had kept alive the memory of his father. When Donald grew to be a teenager, the kidnapper kicked him out in order to find younger boys for the magic worked only with those less than 10 years old.

Donald became a conductor so he could travel far and wide and seek his father.

And so the two men met on the *train* and lived happily ever after.

This story really was written with just the two words in mind and how they might be connected.

You can take 15 to 20 minutes to write your story. (It doesn't have to be so long as the example.) Then read it to the class.

24. Write down either three adjectives or three nouns or a combination and place them in a box or hat. Draw three from the container. If any is a word you wrote, put it back and draw again. Now instead of a story, write a scene that could be part of a play. This means that you use only dialog. You can have three or four days to write it. Then choose as many people as you need to read and act it out in front of the class. If there's time, rehearse the scene a few times before you present it.

25. Have someone write the following general nouns and the following emotions on slips of paper. Put the nouns in one container and the emotions in another.

a. Nouns: *car, planet, scissors, rats, dog, rose, lamp, earth, elephant, bus, toes, book, professor, house, bag, horse, box, tree, mirror, table, rooster, paperweight, bed, chair, stove, bicycle, tree, cloud.*

b. Emotions: *pleasure, hate, awe, love, gladness, serenity, nervousness, anxiety, depression, sternness, cheerfulness, stubbornness, tension, impatience, suspicion, amusement, slyness, arrogance, terror, boredom, excitement, loneliness, happiness, sadness, pity, compassion, humility, pride.*

Each of you should draw both a noun and an emotion. As a character, tell the rest of the class why your noun makes you feel the emotion that you drew. Try to invent a story that makes sense or is logical. For instance, if you drew bicycle and tension, you could make up a story about a bully trying to steal the bike or about not knowing how to use the brake the first time you went for a ride.

26. Have someone in class move you into a certain posture, including a way of holding your legs and arms and body. Keep this pose until you figure out the sort of person it makes you feel like. For example, if your head was bent to one side and your arms were clasped behind your neck, you could be a football player doing calisthenics. You might be feeling nervous because you'll be playing the next day in your first varsity game.

Tell the rest of the class what you feel and why you think you do. Now present a 15-second scene in which, as that person, you talk about your last birthday.

27. Work in pairs.

a. One of you should arrange the other in a certain stance and posture in front of the class. This person then should figure out a logical reason for being in a pose like that and follow through with a motion that will show the class what the movement is. For instance, suppose your partner has you crouch with your right hand extended. You could then pantomime petting a cat or dog or roasting a hot dog around a campfire. Or you could be painting the bottom part of a wall. Now switch who does the arranging.

b. One of you should arrange the other in two separate poses one after the other. Then the task is to go logically from one to the other, showing what job or action you're performing. Suppose, for instance, that the first position is standing on tiptoes, arms spread out at your sides. The second posture is standing with your back arched, leaning backwards. These two positions could go together to show a dive into a swimming pool. Or they could show you stretching just after getting out of bed. Now the second person should be given two poses.

28. Here's the beginning of a story called "An Iffy Situation."

Gladys Hinkle couldn't help it. Every time she was by herself she played the "what if" game. The rules were simple. Take any situation and change it around. The sun always set in the west and rose in the east. Water ran downhill. People grew older. But what if?

What if she were a member of the Boston Celtics? What if she hit her first 30 shots each day but always missed after that?

What if people grew younger instead of older? It would make for an interesting world.

That was the trouble. The world just wasn't an interesting place.

Gladys is in her 20s. She hates her name and her job, feels people take advantage of her, wishes she knew some interesting

59

people and that exciting things would happen. She sets out to change her situation, playing the "what if" game. (This is a game we will come back to several times throughout the rest of the book.) For now, pretend that your name is Gladys Hinkle or if you're male, Grover Hinkle. Like the character in the story, think up some "what if" situations to make your life bearable. As the character, you're capable of making anything happen. The only restriction for this game is your imagination and the fact that you have to do it as the character, not yourself.

Come up with three things you think would make G. Hinkle's life better. Then continue the story from the point the excerpt ends. Playing the character of Hinkle, tell the class what the changes are and how they will make your life better.

29. Each of you should bring some object to class, something that is worth little or no money — like a plastic glass, a burned-out light bulb or a broken toy. Now place all the objects at the front of the room. Think of someone who would logically use one of the objects (but not the one you brought), someone you don't know and to whom the object is very important.

Once you've thought about this, pretend you're the character. Go to the front of the class and pick up the object. First, through how you handle it, show the class how much it means to you. In a few moments tell the story of why this particular thing is so important.

30. Play the word association game. Have someone start with any word and go around the room, each person saying what the previous person's word reminded him or her of. For example: *cat, dog, pet, fleas, litter box, vet, shots, doctor, hospital, nurse, patient, sick, crazy, weird, wonderful, great, fun, play, theatre, act, actress.* End with the person who started.

The important thing to remember is not to block, but to say the first word that comes to mind. The reason is so you get used to letting your imagination and thinking flow without putting stops on them.

This is like brainstorming where no one is to judge the others' responses nor laugh at them. Get used to being in a "safe" environment where it's okay to say things that may otherwise sound dumb or silly.

The only way to be good at something is to experiment; so

don't be afraid to let go and say whatever first pops into your head. It may take a few times before everyone stops laughing or making remarks about others' responses. That is OK until you get used to letting yourself go. If after a few minutes some classmates are still laughing, remember it's because they're the ones who are being judgmental. They're the ones who are afraid to let go.

31. This is very similar, except you actually do brainstorming, which is coming up with ideas about how to do something. Again, the important thing is not to judge the other persons' responses or to react to them other than if they stimulate your own imagination.

The purpose, of course, is to remove restraints from your thinking. So don't be inhibited; say anything that comes to mind. You can use brainstorming with one of the following or other problems that you think of.

 a. What should be done to improve relationships between the younger and older generations?

 b. How can we make sure there's no more war?

 c. How can we improve this school?

 d. What is the best way to involve students in school activities?

 e. What can we do to solve today's drug problem?

32. Imagine a magic merry-go-round. Once you get on, it whirls faster and faster and faster, taking you to an alternate world in a time in the future or past. If you're lucky, you travel to different ages to observe and learn. But occasionally, it drops you in the middle of a Roman amphitheatre or in the cage of a sleeping tiger that you know is going to awaken sooner or later.

You are stuck there until the carousel stops once more to take you back home. Unfortunately, every time you decide to take a ride, the carousel drops its passengers only at times and places of danger.

With a partner, decide where you are, what is occurring and how the two of you can stave off danger till once more you're on the merry-go-round spinning around and around toward home.

Present a one- to two-minute pantomime showing what happened to the two of you. Again, you can exaggerate your actions so there's no doubt what happened. Show the scene from the time the merry-go-round stopped till you jumped on it to come back home.

33. Here's an excerpt from a story called "Mutant." It's a humorous tale that takes place after a nuclear holocaust. Literally everyone, in some way, has mutated, including Milt and Pierre. Keeping in mind that this is a funny story, get together with someone else and discuss what you think happens when Pierre and Milt meet. After you've decided, take a day to prepare a plan or outline to show this. Don't plan out the lines exactly, just the overall idea. Then present a 60-second scene to the rest of the class with one of you playing Pierre, who is a policeman, and the other Milt. It doesn't matter whether a girl or boy plays each role.

Pierre hated the drive home alone at night, and this night was worst of all. The full moon showed pale yellow beyond the smoky clouds. It was a time of insanity, when sleeping beasts began to stir. Or so the legends said. It was a time when hideous mutants rose to stalk the night.

The car began to grumble and dip, and Pierre felt a jolt of fear. He was passing through the jungle, a green tangle of choking vines and undergrowth. It was the forbidden place where only grotesque mutants lived.

The car spit fitfully. Pierre's knuckles formed bands around the steering wheel; his jaw ached from tension. He started rocking back and forth, as if the motion would somehow propel the car forward. With one last gasp the motor died.

* * *

Milt Johnson opened his eyes and stretched. He sighed deeply and sat up. Now the change would begin, the change to power and strength. He held out his hands in front of him and saw them sprout with hair. The fingernails narrowed, hardened into claws. Pads began to form on his palms and fingers.

He felt himself grow as blood surged within him. He tore off his clothes and watched the stiff bristles form on his legs and arms. He began to sniff the powerful odors around him. Odors of must and decay, mixed with animal smells. It was good to be alive. He threw back his head and howled at the moon.

* * *

The worst had happened, and Pierre had to accept it. The decision made, his breath came easier. He checked his gun and undid the latch on the door.

34. Here's an excerpt from a story by Mary Louise O'Hara. It's called "The Mad Countess." After reading this, do one of the following three things:

a. Pretend you're the mad countess. In front of the class pantomime painting a picture of an onion and talk about why you keep painting these pictures.

b. Pretend you're Louis XIV. In front of the class talk about Elise. Tell how you feel about her painting all the pictures of onions and why you think she does it.

c. Present a scene between Elise and Louis in which he tries to persuade her to stop painting onions. Consider the arguments he would use and those she would use.

Each scene should be about 60 seconds long.

At the Versailles Court of Louis the Fourteenth, King of France, the newly wed countess had become an oddity. Courtiers were whispering — when the king or his favorites could not hear — that she must be mad, completely mad.

Elise, the dainty little countess, was painting pictures of onions! Large, small, yellow, pearly, and scallions with long green stems, and she nibbled them constantly.

She sat at an easel in her elegant room, slender fingers, and taffeta gown smudged with charcoal. She drew composition after composition and then painted them slowly.

Elise was the daughter of a renowned scholar, poor but of noble lineage. Their estate lay far from Versailles, but news of Elise's beauty had reached the king's ear, ever sensitive to feminine allurement.

He invited her to enjoy his court and although her father needed her to help with translations, the king's wish was always a command.

35. Choose a partner. One of you should choose which of the following to play:

a. the best-known actor in the world;

b. the most famous scientist;

c. the most popular novelist.

The other will play a writer who is interviewing you for the newspaper that has the largest circulation in the world. Now switch. The interviewer will be the interviewee and vice versa.

Each interview should take two to three minutes.

36. Write a one-page character sketch of the most interesting person you saw today. What makes the person particularly interesting? Exchange your paper with someone else. Now pretend you're the character the other person wrote about. He or she will pretend to be your character.

Go to the front of the class and take turns interviewing each other on what is most important in your life — that is, the life of the character you're portraying.

Learning to Concentrate

Athletes know that to be successful they have to stay focused. The same is true for artists or musicians, and, of course, it's true for people in the theatre.

These exercises are to help you with concentration and focus.

1. Sit in a circle. One person starts by saying: "I'm going on a journey to the Amazon, and I'm going to take along _____." The item should be a noun beginning with the letter "A." Go around the circle. The second person says: "I'm going on a journey to the Amazon, and I'm going to take along _____ and _____." This person repeats what the first person said and adds a noun that begins with the letter "B." The third person names the nouns for the letters "A" and "B" and adds one beginning with "C." Keep going through the alphabet. When anyone forgets one of the nouns, he or she has to drop out. The game continues, even if you have to start through the alphabet a second time, until only one person is left. This last person receives a yellow star.

2. Here's another game you might be familiar with. It's called "Gossip." Break into groups of six or eight and sit or stand in a straight line. The person at one end whispers a sentence to the person next in line. This person in turn passes it to the next person until the last in line hears the sentence. Then he or she has to repeat it aloud. The only rules of the game are that each person has to whisper the sentence and can't repeat it, even if the next person didn't understand. If you don't quite hear the sentence, tell the person on the other side what you think was said. The team that comes up with the same sentence at the end wins. If no one comes up with the exact sentence, the one closest to the beginning sentence is the winner.

3. Everyone should bring a newspaper or news magazine to class. When it's your turn to be "it," a classmate will choose an item of two or three paragraphs for you to read aloud. At the same time, the person who chose the item will read a different news item to you. You'll both begin reading at the same time.

At the end of one minute, your teacher will tell you both to stop reading. You have to give a summary both of what you heard and what you read.

4. Try to count to a hundred by fours while two of your classmates are trying to distract you by whispering fairy tales or nursery rhymes into your ear. After you reach a hundred, say what tales they were telling you.

5. Rub your belly and pat your head; at the end of 10 seconds, pat your belly and rub your head without changing hands; switch again at the end of another 10 seconds.

6. Play a game of charades.

7. Try to learn at least two new things about your best friend when you're together within the next day or two. This should not be things the person tells you, but things you observe. Maybe your friend has an unusual way of walking. Maybe it's something about the way he or she talks that you hadn't noticed before. Do the same thing with one of your family members, someone of a different generation. Make a list of these things.

In two or three days, do a pantomime in class that shows the new things you observed about your friend or one of the others.

8. For the next five days try to see something that you never noticed before. It might be flowers in a yard, a tree or a shrub. It might be a fence you've never noticed or a partially hidden building. On the other hand, it could be something small like a figurine or a picture. Keep a record as you look for these things you haven't previously been aware of:

a. On your way to or from school;

b. On the property next to where you live;

c. Just outside where you live;

d. About the inside of your house or apartment.

Keep a list and tell the class what you discovered.

9. How many different things can you see in the following picture?

Look at it for 30 seconds and then count the number of:

a. Buildings;

b. Vehicles;

c. Trees;

d. Sign posts;

e. Flower containers.

Try this with another picture that your teacher brings to class.

10. Imagine the next stranger you see as having a stuffy nose. Then present a one-minute pantomime of the person duplicating exactly what he or she was doing when you watched. But include the stuffy nose in the pantomime. The rest of the class should tell you how realistic you seemed to be.

11. Here's a list of sentences. With a partner, go to the front of the room. Your teacher will assign you one of the sentences. One of you should say the sentence to your partner, who will respond to you. You, in turn, will then respond to your partner. Keep the exchange going until each person has responded at least five times, which should take about 30 seconds. Keep in mind that you should actually begin talking about what the sentence says or asks. If you disagree with the sentence, try to come up with a good argument. Try to avoid responses of one or two words.

You'll need to pay close attention to each thing your partner says so you'll know the sort of response that is expected.

    a. I love school so much I wish we'd never have vacations.

    b. I think teachers never give us enough homework.

c. Why do you wear your hair like that anyhow?

d. I think television is the dumbest invention ever.

e. I think I'm probably the smartest person in the world.

f. Come on, convince me that you really exist.

g. I think we'd be a lot better off if no one had ever invented the wheel.

h. I'm a Martian in disguise.

i. I don't think anyone should be allowed to get a driver's license until he or she is at least 20 years old.

j. Why shouldn't I eat mud if I want to?

k. No matter what you say, I will not give up my career as an android.

l. If I gave you 20 dollars, would you fly with me to the North Pole and go swimming?

m. My father says that North Americans are the dumbest people in the world.

n. What makes you think you deserve a birthday party?

o. I just hate it when you try to insult me like that.

p. I think that it's okay for little kids to play with matches.

q. Why do you always wear clothes?

r. I think my favorite food in the whole world is pickled grasshopper.

s. I think rock stars are the weirdest musicians ever.

t. I don't understand why you're still afraid of me.

u. What would you do if someone you didn't know came up and simply handed you three dollars and 92 cents?

v. Chicken Little was right; the sky is falling.

w. I don't think anyone should have to work, do you?

x. I haven't slept a wink since I was three years old.

y. I think the importance of being human is highly overrated.

12. For this exercise, you're going to divide into teams.

a. The first team consists only of two members who will play pitch and catch with a baseball and glove, each of which is invisible. This takes concentration because you have to pay attention to exactly where the "ball" is thrown. Catch it and throw it back. Do this just as if the baseball and glove were real. If your partner throws a high pitch, for instance, jump up and get it. If it's wide, stretch for it and so on. Several teams can play at once, depending on how much space you have for the game. Play should continue for about two minutes.

b. This is a little more difficult because one more person is involved. You're to divide into teams of three and play dodge ball. Of course, now the ball is much bigger, about the size of a basketball but almost as light as a beach ball. Begin by choosing who will be first in the center. Play just as if you were using a real ball. Remember that the dodge ball will act a little differently than a baseball because it's bigger and lighter. When one player succeeds in hitting the person in the center, the two of them exchange places. Play the game for three or four minutes.

c. This time you're going to play volleyball, but with fewer players than in regulation games. Divide into teams of four to six for each side of the net. Choose someone to show you exactly how high and how long the net is.

Play this as you would a game with a real ball and net. This means you have to keep your eye on where the ball is going and who is going to hit it. Play for five minutes. The team that is ahead at the end of the time period is the winner.

13. Choose a partner. Each of you will have a turn playing leader and follower. The leader "attaches" an invisible thread around the follower's waist. It's about eight feet long. The leader then draws the follower along by pulling him gently with the thread. It's a magic thread that will ensure that you both get across the quicksand without sinking. But it's very fragile. If it snaps, you can only wave good-bye before you sink forever into the world of Killer Canaries. The Canary King and his court (your classmates) will judge if you've made it across the quicksand (the room) and then back to your starting place without breaking the thread.

14. This is a game called "murder." Sit in a circle. Your teacher will have you choose folded slips of paper from a container. One of these slips has an "M" for murderer. The others have "V" for victim. The object is for the murderer to "kill" all the victims before they catch him or her. The murderer kills the victims by winking at them. As soon as the victims see the murderer wink at them, they have to lower their heads and not make eye contact with anyone else. The victims, while trying not to be killed, attempt to catch the murderer winking at someone else. If they do, they say, "I accuse [*the person's name*] of murder." The victim who solves the murder wins. If no one catches the murderer, he or she wins. If you accuse someone who is not the murderer, the penalty is "death."

15. Do at least two of the following. Walk across the playing area of the class:

a. As an athlete after a mile run;

b. As a girl who just lost out on being a cheerleader;

c. As a young mother carrying her baby in one arm and a bag of groceries in the other;

d. As a well-known movie star walking into a restaurant;

e. As a retired prizefighter;

f. As a 10-year-old whose shoes are too tight;

g. As an 80-year-old out for a stroll;

h. As a teenager walking through the worst section of town at midnight;

i. As a robber escaping from a bank.

Try to make your crosses as realistic as possible. Don't exaggerate or try to be funny.

16. In this exercise you're to tell the class a fairy tale such as "Goldilocks and the Three Bears" or "Jack and the Beanstalk." Begin telling it in English, but when your teacher says, "Switch," you are immediately to begin talking in gibberish. When the teacher calls, "Switch," a second time, go back to English. Try to make both changes without missing a beat. Pretend that the audience understands gibberish as well as English, so speak it as if you expect them to understand. Then when you switch back to English, begin at the same point in the story you might have reached had you told the whole thing in English.

17. Each of you should think of an animal and how it moves. When you're ready, go to the front and begin circling around the playing area as that animal. When others are certain they know the animal you're playing, they can join you. When your herd numbers five, stop. Ask each person with you to write down what the animal was. Have them hold the papers up for everyone to see. Tell them if they were right.

18. For the first part of this exercise, one of you should agree to be the leader; one the follower. In front of the class, the leader pretends to see himself or herself in a mirror. The leader will make various movements, which the follower, his mirror image, should try to match exactly, remembering that the leader's right side is the follower's left and so on. The movements can include gestures, facial expressions and body movements.

71

Try to keep the class from knowing which of you is the leader and which is the follower. Because of this, it might be a good idea to begin by facing each other and placing the palms of your hands together. Make the movements slow and even so it's more difficult to see who is leading and who is following.

Continue the exercise for 60 seconds. At the end the class will vote on who was the leader.

19. This is another mirror exercise. It should be two minutes long. Halfway through, change so that the follower becomes the leader, and the leader the follower. Your teacher will tell you when to change. The vote this time is on who was leading first.

20. Here's another exercise that involves crossing the playing area. You're to pretend that you have something very important to convey to the person who will meet you in the middle. Choose a partner to cross toward you at the same time you're heading toward him or her.

It's up to you to decide what the message is. It can be anything from "I hate you" to "The end of the world has come." It does have to be a complete sentence. The problem is you can use just one word to communicate the sentence. The choice of word is yours. Think about this and the next time you come to class, you can see how well you do with it.

Your partner tries to figure out your message. If he or she does, you get a yellow star! If your partner fails to figure out the message, the class should try.

21. You're to go in front of the class and through any means other than words, portray an emotion. You can do this through facial expression, gestures, stance and movement. Don't over exaggerate or "ham it up." Try to act as natural as possible. You can use the following emotions or others:

a. Rage

b. Fear

c. Love

d. Hate

e. Worry

f. Anger

g. Pity

h. Sorrow

i. Joy

j. Anxiety

As soon as someone else in the class has figured out the emotion, this person should come to the front and portray the same emotion in a different way. This will continue until five different people have portrayed each emotion. Each person should have a turn in being first.

22. Convey a message to the class using any method or combination of methods except verbal language. You can, if you wish, use nonverbalized sounds, such as crying, coughing, sneezing, grunting, snorting and so on. The message, however, can't be funny.

You're to begin at one side of the playing area, travel to the center, stop and face the audience, take no more than five to 10 seconds facing the others, then continue across the stage. The way you cross can be part of the message.

23. Divide into teams of five. Together figure out what you're going to be as you cross the playing area. You all have to be part of the same thing. Examples are a train and a caterpillar. You should hold on to each other in some way and do your best to convey to the rest of the class what you are. Make one complete crossing of the area, and then the other members of the class can guess as you continue to move. You can stop any time, after the first cross, when anyone figures out what you are.

24. Choose a partner and decide on a nursery rhyme. Go to the front of the class. One of you should start the rhyme. After a few lines your teacher will call, "Switch." Without missing a word or a syllable, the person talking stops and the other goes on with the rhyme.

25. Here's another game. You should choose a category such as fruits and vegetables or movie stars. Sit in a circle and in rhythm (4/4 time) 1) slap your thighs, 2) clap your hands, 3) snap the thumb and middle finger on your left hand and 4) the thumb and finger on your right hand. Do that a few times to establish a comfortable rhythm. Suppose you've chosen the category of fruits and vegetables. The first person goes through the four steps of the rhythm and on the final finger snap says something beginning with the letter "A," such as "apricot." Without breaking the rhythm

the next person on the final finger snap says something beginning with "B," such as beet. If you miss, you're out of the game. The person on the other side of you picks up the rhythm with the missed letter and continues. The game goes on, even if it takes more than one time through the alphabet, until only one player is left. He or she wins a yellow star.

26. Your teacher will bring a bagful of miscellaneous objects to school — things that are usually found around the home, in school or in an office. Six people should be on a team.

The teacher will hand an object to one of you, and you pretend it's something else and show this through pantomime. For example, a pencil can become a conductor's baton or a small paint brush. Then hand it to the next person who pretends it's something else. Instead of saying what the object is, pantomime its use.

Be reasonable about it though. The pencil can't become a sword because it is too small. A light bulb can be an ice cream cone but not a globe of the world.

Each group should handle a minimum of five or six objects, each person pantomiming a different use for each.

27. Choose an emotion and a message that go together. For example, "Joy" and "I just won a million dollars." Go to the front

and tell the class the message and convey the emotion. But you can't use words, you have to use numbers. If the first guess about your message is correct, you win a yellow star.

28. Each of you should decide on one very minor change you want to make in the appearance of the room where you meet.

While the rest of the class closes their eyes, one person should make an easily seen but not very apparent change. You have just 20 seconds to do this. When you're finished, the class is to look around and try to discover what you've done. Everyone should write this down. You can turn an object, place a new object unobtrusively and so on.

Each person will make a minor change, and the rest of the class should try to figure out each one and write it down. The person who discovers the most changes wins the game and, of course, a yellow star.

29. The class has just gone to the moon, and you're all exploring the surface. While there, you pick up different objects. They can be real or mythical — such as a piece of cheese or a lunar rock or one of Diana the Huntress' arrows.

You've now collected back outside the rocket ship to show each other your discoveries. The problem is the communication devices in all the spaceships have gone dead. So you have to show in pantomime the objects that you found. Remember that if you make any sudden movements, because of decreased gravity, you may bounce a few feet into the air. So it's much better to use slow motion in showing what each object is and what use it can be put to.

30. Work in pairs. Through actions only, show a relationship between the two of you and how you feel about each other. For example, you could show a coach bawling out a player. The coach could be angry, and the student ashamed or embarrassed.

Think of your own characters or choose one of the following:

a. Best friends
b. Mother/daughter
c. Father/son
d. Father/daughter
e. Mother/son
f. Bully/victim
g. Boss/worker

h. Teacher/student

i. Coach/player

j. Older sibling/younger sibling

k. Set of twins

l. Sales person/customer

m. Director/actor

n. Principal/teacher

o. Teenager/next door neighbor

31. Here again you'll be working with emotions, but you'll not get to choose them ahead of time. The object of the exercise is to take an emotion you draw from a container and pretend you're a character in the following story.

Using what you know about the character from what follows, show the emotion you drew as you think the character would show it. However, you can't use words. Just do it through pantomime, based on clues about the characters in the excerpt. Then take an entirely different character, either from the same scene or a different one and portray the emotion as that character. This time you can use words.

The others in the class are to figure out what emotion you're using and which two characters you're portraying.

This is the opening scene of a science fiction novel, *Death by Stages*. It takes place in the twenty-second century where actors are compelled to take potions to alter their DNA structures so that they become the roles they play. After each performance they change back to themselves. The actors choose the names of well-known performers throughout history.

Will Shakespeare stared into the mirror at a face with furrows deep as ditches, pink scalp sticking through wisps of silken hair. He raised the beaker to his lips and drank. Immediately, the image began to alter into more familiar patterns. No matter how often he went through it, he heaved a sigh of relief with the return of the more familiar self.

Colley Cibber burst through the door.

Will looked over his shoulder. "Why are you always in such a hurry?" he chided.

76

"Dick Burbage of the Duke's Men cannot change back."

Will spun around.

"Tonight Dick played Macbeth and now cannot become himself. His body refuses to alter."

Beads of sweat broke out on Will's forehead. He turned back to the glass. Gone was all trace of King Lear. Before him stood a handsome man in his early 30s. Will closed his eyes and sighed.

"The damned experiments never should have been started in the first place," Cibber said. Twenty-five years old with a pudgy body and an unctuous voice, he was an anomaly. All other actors, so far as Will knew, were able to change to the standard roles using formulas that had been determined a hundred years earlier. Cibber's body wouldn't alter. Will had seen him try the potions, but they never worked.

"What's done is done," Will said. "We can't go back."

"Well, blast it all —"

Suddenly, there was a piercing scream that went on and on.

"What the devil?" Cibber said.

Will jumped up and shoved past him. The other actors milled around in the corridor. Loud sobs came from behind the door on Will's right. That was Marilyn Monroe's dressing room. He knocked, but there was no answer. The sobbing continued.

"Marilyn," he said, "are you all right?"

"Go away."

"Tell me what's wrong." He looked at the others. "Does anyone know why she's crying like that?"

The faces looked blank. Nell Gwyn rushed down the hall toward him. "What is it, Will?" She grabbed his arm. "Has something happened to Marilyn?"

"I don't know." He was afraid to say what was on

77

his mind. Afraid for himself and for Marilyn. But especially for Nell. If anything happened to her, he thought, life would mean nothing. Even if actors couldn't marry, still she was Nell, and he loved her.

Will turned again to the door and pounded. "Marilyn, are you all right?" He turned the doorknob. The bolt was thrown.

"Do something, Will," Nell said.

"Can we break the lock?" It was Michael Chekhov who tonight had played Lear's Fool.

The door opened. Marilyn stood before them, wearing a copy of the dress the original Marilyn had worn in the famous picture over the open vent in New York.

"Oh, my God," Nell said.

Instead of the slightly overweight, black-haired woman the company had grown to love, before them stood Goneril, one of Lear's daughters. "I can't change back," she said, her voice like a little girl's. "What am I going to do?" She threw herself against Will's chest, sobs wracking a body now tall and slender.

"It's all right. Everything's fine," Will said, knowing it wasn't true. Knowing that like the others to whom this had happened there was no changing back. He drew her inside the dressing room and held her tightly against him.

Nell came in, while Will waved for the others to leave.

Nell had once described Marilyn as the kindest person she'd ever met. Why couldn't it be someone else! The thought flitted through Will's mind before he was aware of it, and then he was ashamed.

Marilyn lifted her head and tried to smile. "Oh, Nell."

Cibber weaseled his way through the door. "I'm sorry, Marilyn," he said. "But maybe it's for the best."

Will felt his face grow hot. "What in holy hell is

that supposed to mean?"

"What I said." Cibber stood his ground. "Maybe it's better to stay one way or the other. The changes wreak havoc. We all know that."

Will's anger was replaced by disgust.

"I know it's hard," Cibber continued. "But our lives . . . your lives are shortened. Do you know of any actors who've lived beyond the age of 50?"

"I think you've said enough, Colley," Nell told him. "You'd better leave."

Cibber smiled. "As my lady requires," he said backing out the door.

"I can't stand that man," Nell said, her lips drawn tight.

"He's not so bad." Marilyn tried to smile.

"Only you could say that." Nell's face quickly changed to echo the smile.

32. This is a very prickly situation. Among the cacti is an emissary from an intelligent race out beyond Alpha Centuri.

He has come all this way to bring greetings from himself and his fellow beings. Being the sort of person he is, he thinks he has found the intelligent race on earth. Yet for some reason, they aren't talking. He believes he has interrupted some sort of sacred gathering, much like on his planet, where the beings extend their roots into the ground and silently commune with the whole of their universe.

On earth, of course, the being doesn't understand the local language — or so he believes — and is prepared to wait out the decades or centuries until the cacti wake up and recognize his presence.

Your task is to find the intelligent half plant/half animal and convince him that you're the intelligent one. Your greatest difficulty is going to be that you have to find him first, without damaging him or any of the other priceless cacti in this irreplaceable collection. Get together with a partner and plan what you will do. Your partner will be the alien. You have two days to plan out a four- to six-minute pantomime showing how you solve the problem.

Part III:

IMPROVISATIONS

Using Space

Space can be molded just like clay. Every time we move, we alter space. When we place an object on a table, a wall, the floor or on a stage, we alter space. We change it even by the way we choose to view it. The photographer here chose to present a particular molding of space by camera angle and composition.

Someone else might have shot the scene from behind the trees or across on the other side of the hill. That would have given a different feeling, rather than one of openness.

Even nature molds objects in space to form patterns that are like sculptures.

Look at the following. See how the bridge alters space and suggests a particular mood of tranquility. It seems to be saying, "Follow my path, and I promise you will feel better." It could easily be used for the beginning of an imaginary journey, such as those in Part I.

The design of the book uses space. Look at the way this page is arranged to provide a pleasing picture and to accent the text and illustrations. It leaves margins around and between the lines making it more attractive than if the space were crowded out and the letters were extended from the top edge to the bottom, the left edge to the right.

As a matter of fact, writers often are cautioned to avoid long paragraphs which look like solid blocks of text. Readers like breaks and indentations and other variations. This means that the writer and the publisher have collaborated to sculpt space.

Stores hire artists of a sort to sculpt the space in their windows and display cases. Architects often talk about using space, and so do sculptors.

The way you move is a constant molding of the space around you. You feel uncomfortable if you get too close to strangers or even friends and relatives. Artists are aware of the anxiety and overbearing dominance of crowded space. For example, look at the single griffin that guards the entrance to a now closed art gallery.

From this angle there is a feeling of spaciousness, even more pronounced when you look at the two griffins in relation to each other.

There is more crime and dissatisfaction in crowded areas because there's less space for each person to alter or to mold.

This figure is one of several in an open area amid several artist galleries and shops.

Obviously, the person who arranged the figures realized the importance of sculpting space as well as sculpting the figure, thus allowing for a feeling of openness.

It is important to remember that whether in front of an audience or in everyday life, you are an element in a constantly changing sculpture, comprised of everyone and every object, large or small, within your immediate presence. Most often, you play a big part in determining whether that sculpture is pleasant to look at or if it is ugly.

Of course, the placement undoubtedly has been planned more carefully in this photo. If you will notice the two men on the left and the woman contribute to almost a gentle wave effect, broken by the stiffness of the actor on the right as he obviously reacts negatively to what the others are saying. Even the woman isn't quite as relaxed as the other two men; it's as if she's being pulled in two directions — one exerted by her sons (The play is O'Neill's *Long Day's Journey Into Night*), and by her husband.

You saw by looking at Lesley's drawing on page 44 of birds escaping the frame of the picture that there can be a sense of freedom, and, conversely, a sense of confinement, in a frame or any small area.

Part of performing before an audience is paying attention to how you sculpt space, the constant molding and remolding, often tied in with the mood or subject matter of the piece you're performing.

Scene designers know, for instance, that curving lines in space suggest a lightness and hence a playfulness, whereas sharp angles suggest a somber or heavy quality. It would be inappropriate to present Shakespeare's *Macbeth* in the same space in which you'd present a comedy like Neil Simon's *The Odd Couple* and vice versa. The audience would be confused. Even if they couldn't put a finger on what was wrong, they'd have the feeling that something was.

    1. What moods and feelings are conveyed by these two stage sets, which are similar in a way because they use platforms and levels?

Except when you are alone before an audience, you work with the other performers to sculpt space. So you need to be aware of the pictures you make for an audience.

This also means each other person in your immediate area is entitled to be a co-sculptor of the space. If you get too close, you overpower or destroy the others' sculpture, unless you agree to do the sculpting as one object — such as during an embrace, or when you're holding hands.

2. As an experiment, go to the front of the room with a partner. Stand five or six feet apart. Then very slowly begin to inch toward the other person. Depending on several things, such as how comfortable you feel with the person or how secure you feel about being close to any others, at some point, probably when you are no more than 18 inches apart, you will feel uncomfortable about getting closer. That's okay. Simply stop whenever the feeling is too strong.

As a member of the audience, pay attention to your classmates doing this experiment. You may see some of them leaning backward or exhibiting other signs of discomfort such as giggling or making nervous movements. This happens when anyone attempts to mold the territory, or the globe of space to which every person is entitled.

This is the case with animals as well, who often hurt or kill others who come into their space.

3. The type of character you are playing has a lot to do with the molding of space.

There are two parts to this exercise. First, choose a partner who is to be your spouse. You are to play two characters, one right after the other. Begin by playing a timid man or woman, afraid to express any opinion or in particular disagree in any way with your spouse. Next pretend you are a ruler of the mightiest kingdom on earth, a kingdom you have put together by overpowering other nations and stealing their land, a ruler so mighty that virtually everyone is afraid of you.

In this improvisation, your job as both of these characters, one after the other, is to explain to your partner why you did not arrive home as expected. In both instances, the spouse was expecting to go with you to an important banquet.

Your spouse cannot use words to show displeasure, but can

use any other means except touch of any sort. No matter how your spouse reacts, you are to give a one-minute explanation of why you came home late.

Later, the class will talk about the differences in the way the two of you molded space.

The next few exercises are to have you begin changing your thinking about the properties of space and how it can be molded.

4. Decades ago, taffy pulling parties were popular. This is where those present took a big piece of taffy in both hands and then stretched it, so it would cool and harden as air touched its surface. You won't pull taffy, but you will pull space. Stretch your arms straight out in front of you, and grab a hunk of space in both hands. Gently pull your hands apart, stretching it. Visualize the space as you stretch it into long strands. Now fold up these strands, squeeze them together in one piece and stretch the space once more.

The idea, of course, is to have you see the plasticity of space, the way it can be shaped and molded.

5. Take the same bit of space or a different one you grab from somewhere near you and squeeze it gently into a lump in both hands. The lump should be about the size of a baseball. Roll it between palms and fingers until you can see it is perfectly round and smooth. Open your hands and watch it take its old shape as part of the whole.

6. This is a two-part exercise.

a. Form your hand into a fist and hold it out in front of you. See how the space molds itself around you. Now think of space molding itself around your head. Spread your legs and feel it around the ankles, the calves, the thighs. Close your eyes for a moment and imagine the space.

b. The space is eager to mold itself effortlessly around you when you move. Instead of feeling the space around you, this time feel yourself molding the space. Stretch your arms out to the sides and mold the space so that it becomes sleeves. Relax your arms, then lift one leg for a moment, molding the space around it. Now mold the space with your other leg. Think of it in the same way you would of making a plaster cast.

Finally, swing your arms or your feet in any patterns you wish and see how quickly the space is molded. This is the sort of thing you do any time you move.

7. In this exercise, choose three of the following and decide how each would mold and re-mold their space. Think about this until you've figured out the appropriateness of the moldings. Now go to the front of the room and cross the stage three times, once as each of the characters you've chosen. Then have the class figure out which of the characters you chose and the order of presenting them. If you were absolutely convincing on each one, you deserve a big yellow star!

a. A grandparent suffering from arthritis;

b. A soldier who's just finished basic training;

c. A rookie policeman stalking his first thief;

d. A child chasing a balloon;

e. A person of late middle-age chasing a UFO;

f. A postal employee heading home just after making rounds;

g. A teenager headed to a new school for the first time;

h. A mother rushing to see her child at the hospital emergency room;

i. An athlete walking home after a big defeat;

j. A person headed for the first day at a new job;

k. Someone who's just been fired from a job;

l. A teenager who just demolished the new family car;

m. An elderly person on the way to the hospital to visit a friend;

n. A person who's just been told to come to the adoption agency to pick up a new baby;

o. A student who's just received an A+ instead of an expected F.

8. This is similar to an earlier exercise but with a slight difference. All of you together will move around the room, each gradually becoming your favorite animal, molding space as only you can. This should take you about a minute. When you're finished, draw a picture of how at least a portion of the mold — but not the animal — looked when you molded it.

One by one go in front of the class and show your drawings; don't worry about how well you draw. Have each try to figure out what type of animal you were.

9. Divide into groups of eight or 10. In turn, each team should go to the playing area and arrange itself in a pleasing sculpting of space. Then slowly each of you on the team should transform yourself into a piece of playground equipment, doing whatever it is the equipment does, like swinging, spinning or sliding. It's okay if more than one person becomes a particular thing.

10. Rube Goldberg machines are those which perform a lot of actions, with only one result. In this exercise, you are to split into groups of eight to 10 (or less depending on the size of your class). In each group, one person should go to the front of the room and perform an automated movement like a part of a machine. One by one the rest of you in the group should add on to that machine. It doesn't matter whether you have a purpose or an end product. Just perform each action in a rhythm that fits in with everyone else's.

11. Become part of a work crew. This cannot be planned out, so you won't divide into teams. This can be any logical work crew,

the type you might see any day in any area. It could be a group cleaning up litter or doing construction work.

One of you should think of an idea and go up and start "working." One by one others join you when they realize what you're doing. Each crew should consist of five or six members, and no member can do exactly the same thing as any other.

Keep in mind that the purpose of the exercise is to mold space in a logical and pleasing way.

12. Divide into teams of two; decide on a task that it takes two people to do, such as moving a heavy piece of furniture. You can have a couple of minutes to figure out the task and to talk about how you'll do it. Then in pantomime, being as precise as you can, perform it for the class. If you use imaginary objects, make sure to establish their shapes and keep them the same throughout. For instance, don't let a piece of furniture become first a dining chair and then a big overstuffed chair.

When you're finished, the rest of the class should be able to tell you immediately what you were doing.

13. This exercise is called "getting there." The idea is that you've come out of one room or building and are headed for another. Through the way you mold space, that is, movement of whatever types you want to use, you must convey to the class where you have been and where you are going. For instance, it could be from the bedroom to the living room before leaving for school.

When you exit the first place, you have a minute to get to the next. You can take a shorter time than that, but no shorter than 30 seconds. It's all right if you want to make one or more stops in between.

At the end of the improvisation, the class should have been able to figure out the two places and why you were going from one to the other.

14. This exercise is called "being there."

   a. You are to convey through any type of movement where you are. At one of the following:

      1) An art museum;

      2) The courtyard of an elegant house;

      3) A sidewalk cafe;

93

4) At a fountain in the park;

5) Walking along a trail in the woods;

6) A rose garden.

Do a one-minute improvisation showing the class which of these six places you are visiting and how you feel about being there.

b. Do the same thing, with a location of your own choosing. It can be any place, inside or out, at any time of day or year. Have the class try to figure out where you were.

15. In this improvisation, you are to think of someone well-known, either real or imaginary like Superman or Groucho Marx. But it should be a human being, not an animal. You should think how to convey who this is without actually saying it. You will be performing this with someone else, but you aren't allowed to ask each other questions beyond things like: "How are you?"

The idea is that you have gone for a stroll in the park and have come to a barrier. The park beyond the barrier is closed for some reason but will open in five or 10 minutes. You decide to wait. You can either sit on a park bench or stand.

You start to talk about why this portion of the park is closed and how you feel about it. Through your conversation with each other, it should become apparent who you are.

Once you are sure who the other person is, just say, "I know you." But you should continue to talk until each partner "recognizes" the other. Then, still without revealing names or other information that would tell definitely who you are, you switch roles. The second part should continue for one minute.

At the end, see if each of you was right about the other.

Your teacher will pick the pairs that will perform together.

16. Mimes often make space appear as visible as solid objects. Here's an exercise you may have seen performed on television by a mime. Pretend you're confined in a small box and are trying to get outside. Make the box appear real to the class. You can have two or three days to practice the pantomime before you present it to class. It should be about three minutes.

17. In this exercise, all you have to do is play a game of tag. No more than six people should play in each game. The only difficulty is that you have to play in slow motion. Otherwise, make the game real. Choose someone to be "it." Then stay only in the playing area. The person will try to tag you, but you will try to escape. Anyone who doesn't continue in slow motion will be warned the first time and ejected from the game the second time.

Continue to play for two minutes. Then let another team play. Those who watched will talk with each team about how realistic the game appeared and what could have been done to improve it.

18. Here's an exercise to do by yourself. You've lost your wallet somewhere in the living room; you need it or you won't be able to buy your lunch, and you've already skipped breakfast.

The living room is in the playing area, but the furniture and any other objects are invisible. In your own mind establish exactly where things are, so if you need to, you can come back several times to the coffee or end table or to look under the cushions of the sofa or chair. Keep the objects and the space consistent, and make your search realistic. Take two minutes to look for your wallet; end by either finding it or giving up.

19. This will test both your concentration and your ability to mold space. Go into one of the following invisible rooms: the kitchen, the bedroom, the living room, the dining room or the basement. Build a sequence of actions in which you logically use at least six objects from the room. There has to be a logical reason for what you do. For instance, in the kitchen you could:

a. get the lemon from the refrigerator,

b. cut it in two with the knife from the drawer or knife rack,

c. get a pitcher,

d. squeeze the lemon into it,

e. add sugar,

f. add water,

g. get ice cubes and add them to the pitcher,

h. stir the drink,

i. get a glass, pour the lemonade and drink it.

Do this same thing using a second room and different objects.

20. You and a partner are intelligent robots; that is, you can speak and understand others. However, your programming cannot be altered except by the person who owns you.

One of you is owned by the woman of the house, the other by the man. The woman has told the one she owns that she definitely wants the furniture rearranged. The man has told the one he owns that under no circumstances is anything in the living room to be moved.

You both meet in the living room; one of you is trying to move the furniture; the other wants it left where it is. Talk to each other and use any arguments you can. The only thing you should agree on ahead of time is what and where each piece of furniture is.

One of you should enter from Stage Right (the actor's right facing the audience) and the other from Stage Left (the actor's left facing the audience).

Your scene should last for about 60 seconds. Instead of just stopping, however, you have to bring this to some sort of conclusion.

21. This time you are marionettes. Throughout this pantomime, you have minds of your own and won't listen to the one who holds your strings. Yet the person does his best to control you.

At the same time the two of you are having a disagreement with each other. Mr. Marionette wants to go to the championship croquet game where your little dummy son is playing; Ms. Marionette wants to go to a rally being held to demand puppet freedom, with no strings attached.

Not only do Mr. and Ms. Marionette argue with each other, but they also have to contend with the person who's trying to control their strings.

Make your movements and actions fit the situation, and bring the piece to a satisfactory resolution of some sort within two minutes.

22. Two of you are at a sporting event. It's up to you to decide what it is and through your actions (but no words) let the audience know.

You both are enjoying the event except when you discover you are rooting for opposite sides. Then you have a confrontation.

You should continue this confrontation until one of you realizes that the other is a good friend you haven't seen in almost 10 years.

Take it from there and improvise a scene of two minutes in which you accomplish these four goals.

a. To show what the event is;

b. To confront each other;

c. To recognize each other;

d. To bring about a resolution.

23. You did something really dumb, and because of it, you're in big trouble. What was it, and how are you going to get out of it?

For instance, it could be something like accidentally throwing the car keys into a street-side mailbox, and you have to be somewhere in 10 minutes for the most important interview of your life.

Do this only through actions without words. The scene should last about 90 seconds.

The next few exercises deal with space and also lead into the next section that deals with conflict.

24. Work in pairs. You are to engage in a sword fight, using imaginary swords. But you are to disagree about something which you decide on beforehand.

The argument and sword fight should last 90 seconds to two minutes. Each of you should go on the offensive and the defensive at various times. That is, both of you could seem to be winning or losing at different times.

As you fight with the imaginary swords, argue your points for or against whatever it is you choose as your subject.

The purpose of this improvisation is to show you how to be both aggressive and submissive with your body, as well as your voice. Pay attention to how you use space to do this.

It doesn't matter who wins the disagreement. The important thing is to make both the verbal and physical battles realistic.

25. Work in pairs. Both of you are aliens from different planets, trying to pass as earthlings. But you know very little about the planet except how to speak English and how to look — the latter because both of you are excellent shape changers.

Entering from opposite sides of the playing area, you meet in the center. Each now wants to find an earthling who will help you understand local customs and laws. You are relieved to spy each other because each thinks the other alien is a native of earth.

The idea is that you want to gain as much information as you can so you can adapt to living on earth. At the same time, you don't want to give away the secret that you're merely here to observe this strange and weird race called human beings.

The improvisation should last approximately three minutes, and you should bring about some sort of satisfactory conclusion.

26. Mimes such as Marcel Marceau often exaggerate their actions or make them bigger than life. This is so the audience will be sure to understand what they are doing, and it's also to make the action funnier.

For this activity there are few rules or boundaries. You are to be a mime, presenting a series of activities that leads to some conclusion — like getting ready for a big night out when everything goes wrong, or trying your best to get a job done that refuses to stay done, such as stacking cans. You are to bring the scene to a conclusion of some sort. This time it can be humorous and exaggerated. You smash the cans so they're flat, you nail them to the floor or each other, you shoot them.

In other words, the scene should show you having conflict or difficulty with whatever it is that you're trying to do.

Take a week or 10 days to plan this and present it. It should last about three minutes.

27. On pages 101 and 102 are photos of three different locations. The first is a city that is slowly becoming less solid, a city that is turning into mist. Only you and your partner can keep this from happening. If you fail, everything you love and know will dissipate with it. A witch holds you captive behind these bars.

She has placed a curse of fog upon the land, your native country, just beyond the hill. Even if you escape the prison that leads to the enchanted yard, guarded by the slate monolith that turns into a deadly killing machine, you still have to find your way to the other side of these petrified vines to the magic door.

Once through the door, you have reached safety for the witch has no control there. She used all her power in cursing your country and has gone to sleep for two hundred years, leaving only the castle itself to guard you. So confident was she of her power, that she gave you the antidote to the curse. All you have to do is say the magic words, and your home and land will be safe.

You can use props or furniture to simulate the bars, the killing machine, the vines and door and finally the city you have to reach. The two of you working together should come up with a way to get out of prison and back home. You can have two weeks to plan this out. Then in a four- to five-minute pantomime, show how you outwit the witch and save your country.

Building Scenes

Some of the pantomimes and improvisations you've done so far have involved conflict, a problem that has to be solved before the scene can be brought to a satisfactory conclusion. For example, the two robots are opposed because their goals are directly opposite each other. This means that the basis of the conflict is these opposing forces.

Conflict is the basis of most plays and most fiction. Forces clash and a struggle continues until one of them is overcome. However, the opposition that provides the conflict doesn't always have to be another person. It can be the environment or surroundings such as the person's losing the car keys in the mailbox or not being able to find a wallet.

In this section you will be working with improvisations that have some sort of conflict that has to be resolved before the scene can reach a logical conclusion.

1. This exercise is more involved than any you have done yet. It includes a lot of conflict, the clash of good and evil in a battle over a royal heir.

An alabaster lion guards the steps to this house. Inside is the heir to the throne, kidnapped as a baby and kept prisoner until two of the ablest subjects of the land come to pit their strength and intelligence against the awesome power of the evil magician who holds the child prisoner. Can they outwit him? Not without a struggle, for there are problems they first must overcome. Anyone trying to go up the steps awakens the lion who turns to flesh and blood. Most likely, he hasn't eaten in days! How will they get past the lion and the magician, intent on developing further evil spells to prevent the royal child's rescue? What will the magician do to prevent the rescue? What will the heir do to help?

One of you should play the heir, two the rescuers, one the lion and another the magician. You can have at least a week to get together and plan an outline of what happens. Remember that it's possible that the magician could outwit the would-be rescuers or that they could be eaten by the lion. Take two weeks to plan a scene that pits the rescuers and the heir against the magician and the lion and present it as an improvisational scene of six to eight minutes.

2. In the scene that follows, excerpted from "Fitting the Mold," it is obvious that the conflict between Kevin and Zach has gone on for a long time, probably years. It started after Kevin's mother died; Kevin felt that Zach didn't do as much for her in her last days as he should have. Kevin was 12 at the time; he's now 19. The father and son drifted further and further apart until Kevin began using the back entrance, which opens directly into his room. It's been a couple of years since he's even gone into the rest of the house. Pete, visiting Zach, sees the door open and looks in at Kevin's aquarium. Kevin invites him in.

KEVIN: **Hi, I'm Kevin. Zach's son.**

PETE: **Pete Williamson. A friend of your dad's from Ohio.**

KEVIN: **Yeah, well, Dad and I pretty much try to stay out of each other's way.** *(PETE crosses right to the aquarium.)* **I've never had luck with angels. For a long time nothing worked for me except guppies. I must have got the balance right or something.** *(He crosses Up Right of PETE.)* **You're from Ohio, you say?**

PETE: **I used to live in Manhattan.**

KEVIN: **You must have met Dad when you lived here before?**

PETE: No, actually, I didn't. He wrote to me about —

KEVIN: Oh, well, it's none of my business. Unfortunately, damn it, nothing's my business where Dad's concerned. Sometimes, I wish things were different. *(Looking into PETE's eyes)* Dad can be a great guy, but we always get off on the wrong foot, it seems. Sometimes I wish . . .

PETE: I'm sorry.

KEVIN: Hey, it's not your problem.

PETE: Thanks for letting me see the fish.

KEVIN: Any time.

(PETE crosses Stage Left and steps out of KEVIN's room, closes the door and crosses to the kitchen. As the lights come up, ZACH is at the counter fixing a salad.)

ZACH: Did I hear you talking to someone?

PETE: Kevin.

ZACH: *(Turning; surprised)* What?

PETE: His door was open. He saw me looking at his aquarium and invited me in.

ZACH: Quite an honor. He hasn't invited me in since God knows when.

PETE: He acknowledged that you aren't on the best of terms.

ZACH: I'll bet he said it was all my fault.

PETE: He didn't say much of anything.

ZACH: I guess things have gone on too long to do much about it. I'm not even sure I want to now. Terrible thing to say, isn't it? You know what I wish? *(Shakes his head.)* Oh, hell, there's no point in talking about it. Damn!

As you see, this conflict is still there, probably less intense than it once was but unresolved. Yet both Zach and Kevin indicate they wish they could end it.

Knowing only this much about the characters, what do you think could be done to resolve the situation?

Get together in groups of three, one for each of the three

105

characters, and come up with an outline for a scene in which Zach and Kevin, with Pete's help, resolve their differences. It probably would be a stronger scene if they start out in direct conflict.

Once you've finished the outline present a three-minute scene in which the conflict is resolved. You can change the sex and names of the characters, if you wish.

Any story or scene that has conflict begins with what is called an *inciting incident*. This is where the conflict starts. The character accidentally throws the keys into the mailbox; the two robots have been given opposite goals; the two members of the crowd at the sporting event discover they are rooting for opposite teams.

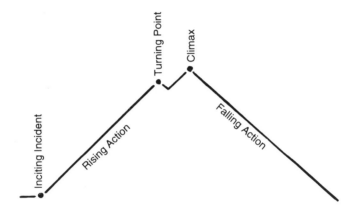

The conflict continues to build. The person who threw away the keys becomes more frantic about not getting to an appointment, or each robot is becoming so angry and upset it will do anything to follow its owner's orders. This part of the scene is called the *rising action* because it does rise in intensity. The complication or problem intensifies, which causes the suspense to build. Will the person be able to retrieve the keys or not? Will he or she win over the opposition or be defeated?

The suspense and conflict build until it's easy to see that one side or the other will win. This is called the *turning point*. It's the place where the character knows whether or not the problem can be solved. The point at which the character wins or loses is the *climax*, the high point of the scene, which usually ends pretty quickly afterwards.

Most of the time a scene can be more interesting if the audience knows the character's reason for the conflict. An example is the appointment for the person who lost the keys, or the fact that the robots' owners demanded that they follow directions and they have no choice but to try as hard as they can.

Finding Intentions

Many scenes or situations can have a different reason behind them for reaching a certain goal. This reason is called the *intention*, which is the motivation behind why a character wants something, why he or she is determined to reach a certain goal. The intention can be just as important as the fact that the person wants to reach the goal. For the same set of circumstances, there can be any number of intentions, depending on the type of person a character is and the circumstances that led him or her to this point.

As an example, various movies and novels have been based on the idea that a group of people are gathered in a certain location to try to beat out others for a big reward — usually a lot of money. One person may want the money to be able to pay for surgery for a child who will die without it. Another may want to escape living in a slum area. A third may want to be able to send a dying mother on one last trip to visit relatives. There can be as many reasons for trying to win the prize as there are participants in the contest. Yet the obvious goal is the same — to win the prize.

3. Work in pairs. Choose one of the following. Figure out a logical intention for each character, and present a 90-second improvisation showing the opposition. Bring the scene to some sort of conclusion. Remember that no intention is wrong so long as you can make it sound natural and realistic. In situation "a," for instance, one could want them to impress a boss who's coming to dinner; the other could think they should save the money to pay an overdue bill. Or one wants the crystal glasses to replace those destroyed in a fire, and the other already has bought a set as a surprise.

    a. A married couple in a department store. One wants to buy a set of very expensive crystal glasses. The other doesn't.

    b. Two young kids. One wants to explore an abandoned house; the other is very much against it. Both have heard that the house is haunted.

c. Two high school students who very much like a particular sport. One wants more than anything to try out for it if the friend will; the other just as strongly believes neither should try out for it.

d. Two teenagers on a date. One very much wants to see a certain movie that is closing that night; the other wants to go hear a singer who will be in town for only one day.

e. A parent and a teenager disagreeing on the type of shoes to buy for gym class.

f. A commander-in-chief and his general disagreeing on whether to attack the opposition at night.

g. Two people disagreeing on who should drive to the mall.

h. A parent and child disagreeing on whether the kid's allowance should be doubled.

i. An engaged couple, one of whom wants a tattoo; the other is strongly opposed to it.

j. One person is demanding that the other come to where he or she is standing; the other person is strongly opposed to it.

Choose one of these scenes and present it, showing the intention and the actual struggle on each side to reach the opposing goal. Now take the same scene and present it with an entirely different set of intentions.

4. In a previous section, you learned about the "what if game," as played by G. Hinkle. Here are some examples of situations that can arise from this.

a. What if you walked into this class tomorrow and you didn't know either the other students or the teacher?

b. What if you walked into this class tomorrow and your teacher was sitting in your seat and everyone thought you were the teacher?

c. What if you went home from school today and your family could neither hear you nor see you?

    d. What if you went home from school today and your family wouldn't let you in?

    e. What if you went on a class picnic, and suddenly nothing looked familiar, and so you were lost and couldn't find out how to get home?

    f. What if you went on a class trip to a zoo and one of the zookeepers tried to capture you and put you in one of the cages?

Pick one of these situations and play the central character, choosing any of your classmates you need for it. Work out the intentions before you begin and tell the others what they are.

5. It's not at all difficult to come up with "what if " situations. The only rule is that you take a real situation that stays exactly the same except for one aspect. It's this one thing that bends everything out of shape, that seems even more weird in that everything else is the same as always.

For this exercise, come up with a "what if " situation of your own that you think would be fun to do. It doesn't matter how many people are involved, but you will play your own central character.

Choose others to be in the improvisation. Remember that there should be conflict. Your goal should be to make things "right." You can do this however you want. You can try to think of a logical reason for what has happened. In example "c," for instance, your family may be ignoring you because they've been hypnotized by a creature from space who plans to kidnap them but doesn't realize there's another family member, you. While they were under hypnosis, he told them that they would be going with him to collect something they've always wanted, so that they can think of nothing else.

Assign others in the class to play the different roles in your "what if " situation and present it to the class in a five- to six-minute scene.

6. Choose a historical figure you know about or can easily research, such as Teddy Roosevelt or Elizabeth I. You may play the same one you used in Part I if you wish.

Get together with a partner who has chosen a different

character. Both of you have been able to travel to the future (our present). Suppose that you meet in the lobby of the local library where you have both been reading newspapers about contemporary life. You introduce yourselves. When you realize you both are from other time periods, you agree that your own time was much better than the present, but each of you tries to convince the other that your own time period was the best in which to have lived. Do your utmost to convince the other person you are right. Present this in an improvisation of three to four minutes.

7. Choose a partner for this exercise. Here's how it starts. You say: "I didn't know what to do when [*something happened*]. What would you have done?"

Your partner answers: "Well, I would have [*done such and such*]."

You reply: "Some help you are," which begins the conflict which has to be resolved.

Here are a couple of examples:

a. That silly alligator rubbed against my leg and wanted me to take him home.

b. The bride insisted I come along as chaperon on the honeymoon.

Think of other examples and write out one or two. Your teacher will collect them. You'll draw one of them and read it to your partner. The partner will give you advice that is totally ridiculous, which is what starts the conflict that intensifies when you say: "Some help you are." This, of course, makes your partner angry.

Keep the scene going for about a minute and then in some way resolve it.

8. Divide into groups of four or five. This is the situation: A funny elephant has escaped from the zoo while you and your friends are there.

Each person in your group wants to do something different about this for the following reasons:

a. When the elephant is out of his enclosure, he tells the most wonderful jokes and makes people laugh hysterically.

110

b. He has to be caught because he's very valuable and there's a reward.

c. He bites.

d. He's always sad when he's in his enclosure.

e. The cage is to protect him from other wild elephants who are jealous of his sense of humor.

f. He's very lonely for his family back in the country where he was captured.

You are the only people who can do anything about the situation. What do you do? With three or four others, talk about it as you listen to his jokes. Bring this to a resolution in two to two-and-a-half minutes.

9. Here are a number of situations for an improvisation involving just two people. Get together with a partner and choose the one you like best. Then do a two-minute improvisation.

a. One person has just won a big award; the person's best friend, expected to win, came in last.

b. On the day you are to move after two years in the area, the person next door says he or she finally has planned a big party to welcome you to the neighborhood.

c. You are so excited you can hardly wait to tell your new neighbor about the wonderful job you just got. During the course of the conversation, you discover that this person was fired from the job you're getting.

d. You are in a foreign country where you've never been before. You don't speak the language, and you just realized that you've lost the address of your hotel. You try to ask directions of someone you meet on the street. This person tries to tell you that he (or she) just lost his hotel's address and is from still a different country. Neither of you speak the other's language.

10. Six people are needed for each of the following. The first pair will start and then will be replaced in 30 seconds when the second group takes over. The third pair takes over in 30 more seconds. Everyone should have a chance to begin and end one of the scenes.

111

a. An irate neighbor has come to complain that you're playing your music too loud.

b. A neighbor's dog has gotten loose and has chewed up your flower bed.

c. You complain to a neighbor about the couple's son spray painting the side of your house.

d. A friend has let you take the blame for breaking a large window in the school auditorium.

e. Your brother or sister has stuck you with three days' worth of dirty dishes just before your folks are due home from a very unsuccessful business trip.

f. You catch a co-worker stealing from the cash drawer.

11. You could treat many of the improvisations up to this point in a humorous way. However, those that follow deal with serious problems. You should not make light of them. Do try to bring about a sort of resolution. The improvisations should be a minimum of three minutes and a maximum of five.

a. A 15- or 16-year-old acquaintance tells a friend of plans to run away from a home situation that is unbearable.

b. A student tells a close friend about finding out the perfect way to cheat on exams, a way that has brought high grades all year.

c. One person asks another for advice on what to do about being sexually harassed at work.

d. One friend tries to convince another he or she has a severe eating disorder, either bulimia or anorexia.

e. A person tells a friend life isn't worth living because of not being able to meet parents' expectations.

f. Someone tells a friend of suffering severe physical abuse at home but wants the friend to promise not to tell anyone.

g. A teenager tries to convince a friend to get help for an uncontrolled temper.

h. A confrontation takes place between two students, one of whom is a bigot, who keeps harassing a new classmate.

12. Try to come up with similar situations as those in the last exercise. Then use them as the basis of an improvisational scene of three to five minutes. In class you might bring up different situations to discuss.

13. Following are scenes from three plays. In each the problem or conflict has just been introduced. Figure out what you think could logically happen after this. With a classmate, make a brief outline in which you bring about a resolution to the problem. Then present a three- to five-minute improvisation showing the way you've worked out for the play to end.

a. The name of this play is "Ties." This is the beginning scene. Tom has just come home after being hospitalized, the result of a serious heart attack. His friend Frank is there to help him through the first few days till he's able to do things for himself.

FRANK: *(From Off-stage)* **Can I get you anything, Tom?**

TOM: No, I'm fine.

FRANK: Would you like to go out for lunch?

TOM: I really don't think so . . .

FRANK: Dr. Stephens said it's OK. If you don't overdo.

TOM: I'd rather stay home.

FRANK: It'll do you good. I thought we'd go to the Valencia.

TOM: I don't have any appetite. *(FRANK enters Stage Left wiping his hands on a dish towel.)*

FRANK: Going to give up and die?

TOM: I just don't want to go out for lunch.

FRANK: We could go somewhere else.

TOM: I don't want to go anywhere else. I want to stay home.

FRANK: I want what's best for you. And if that's staying home and moping, fine. *(He turns to leave.)*

TOM: God, Frank, I'm not moping.

b. This excerpt is from a children's play, "Dana and the Monster." As you see, the names Dana and Linn could be used both for boys or girls. This is the opening.

113

MONSTER: Boo!

DANA: Oh, hi.

MONSTER: Aren't you afraid of me?

DANA: Should I be?

MONSTER: Everybody is.

DANA: Everybody?

MONSTER: Well, sort of. I try to scare people, but I'm not really successful.

DANA: I can understand that. I'm not successful either.

MONSTER: My name is Xyssth. You can call me Linn.

DANA: I'm Dana. *(They shake hands.)* So where are you from?

MONSTER: The other side of the moon.

DANA: There's no air there. You couldn't breathe.

MONSTER: Not your moon. Another one far, far away.

DANA: Uh huh.

MONSTER: It's true.

DANA: Why did you try to frighten me?

MONSTER: I want to live on Xyllt.

DANA: What's Zill . . . whatever you said?

MONSTER: A planet. Like earth. But everyone is so scary there that — I don't think you'd understand.

DANA: Yes, I would.

MONSTER: You have to be scary to live there. So everyone has to take a test for scaring people. And if you don't succeed, you live on the moon forever. It's lonely, away from moms and dads and cousins. It's ever so much better on Xyllt.

DANA: It seems like you have a problem. But doesn't everyone?

MONSTER: Do you?

DANA: Back home I had friends. But nobody likes me here. They say I talk funny. 'Cause I have an accent.

MONSTER: Maybe they just have to learn to know you.

DANA: You think it's easy to make friends?

MONSTER: We're talking, aren't we? Everyone becomes

my friend, and I can't scare anyone.

DANA: I wish I had your problem. Nobody wants to be my friend.

This is an excerpt from "Sounding Brass." This scene takes place just after Martin's father has tried to strangle him. His mother's intervention has possibly saved his life. It's December and very cold. Martin ran out of the house and walked to the town where he used to live to see former neighbors whom he always liked. Martin is 17 years old. As the scene opens, Martin is pounding on the door. Liz lets him in.

LIZ: Marty! What in the world are you doing here?

MARTIN: I . . . uh, oh, God, Liz.

LIZ: Come on in. Burleigh's not here. He's down at the VFW.

MARTIN: May I have a drink of water?

LIZ: Of course. Sit down. *(MARTIN sits at the kitchen table as LIZ crosses to the cupboard for a glass. She opens the refrigerator, takes out a pitcher, pours the water and hands it to MARTIN.)* Is something the matter, Martin?

MARTIN: He tried to kill me, Liz. I thought he was going to do it.

LIZ: Who! For God's sake, who?

MARTIN: My father. Dan. *(He takes a long swallow and sets the glass down.)*

LIZ: I don't understand.

MARTIN: He was choking me, trying to strangle me.

LIZ: I can't believe that.

MARTIN: He was.

LIZ: You must be mistaken. I know your father better than that.

MARTIN: Do you?

LIZ: Of course. You're probably drawing something totally insignificant way out of proportion.

MARTIN: *(Standing)* Thanks for the water. *(He crosses to the door.)*

115

LIZ: Wait, Martin, please.

14. There are many other sources you can draw on for improvisations. A good one is well-known sayings. Although the conflict isn't stated in them, it's often implied. For instance, let sleeping dogs lie, can suggest that someone digs up something that should have remained buried and now has to suffer the consequences. Take one of these sayings and, with a partner, come up with a way to build a scene that includes conflict.

a. A fool and his gold are soon parted.

b. Don't put the cart before the horse.

c. Don't rob Peter to pay Paul.

d. You can't have your cake and eat it, too.

e. Pride goeth before a fall.

f. Don't judge a book by its cover.

g. A little knowledge is a dangerous thing.

h. Too many cooks spoil the broth.

i. Don't put all your eggs in one basket.

j. Prevention is the best cure.

Think of a situation where someone didn't pay attention to the advice offered in one of these sayings. Figure out the conflict and the problem this caused, and then work this into a two- to three-minute improvisation. You can try to think of other sayings, if you like.

Learning to Build Characters

Think of plays, movies or TV shows, and you probably think first of the people in them. So it is important to be able to create characters who are real and memorable. This section is to begin acquainting you with the idea of building good characterizations.

1. This old schoolhouse in rural Pennsylvania was built in the late 1800s.

As a young child, you attended this school from 1912 till you finished sixth grade. Think back over your life and reflect about what it was like back then, particularly attending this old one-room schoolhouse.

You have three days to come up with the story of your life from the age of six through the age of 11. Take two to three minutes to tell the rest of the class about it.

You already are acquainted with the idea of keeping a file on which you jot down traits and mannerisms of people you see every day. This is an excellent idea you can continue so long as you do improvisations or acting.

It's a good idea actually to get a file box that holds three-by-five cards. Then keep a record of different types of people you see and what makes them individuals. You might set it up something like this.

> *Teenager/Male*
> *Dirty, torn clothing. Unshaved*
> *Begging outside the Mall*
> *No coat or sweater - Looks cold.*
> *(over)*
>
> *Kept scrunching up his face. He tried to smile, but just looked defiant. He could have been handsome. It was funny, but in different circumstances, I felt he'd be a good friend.*

It is a good idea to get into the habit of doing at least one card a day for your file. Then you might want to divide the file into different sections, referring to sex and age, such as Young Man, Middle-aged Woman and so on. Set up the categories in the way that works best for you. But do include people of both sexes since you may be able to use interesting traits from either.

2. At the end of each week you should have at least five new cards in your file. A week from today tell the class about each person you have made a card for in the past seven days. Tell which you think is the most interesting and why. Tell which one you think has the most unusual trait.

3. Take two of the characters from someone else's file box and imagine them together in an elevator that's stuck between floors. With someone else, prepare a one-minute pantomime showing the two characters' actions and feelings. Remember to base this as closely as you can on the people you heard described.

4. Get together with a classmate and have that person tell you about two or three characters in his or her file. Then explain what you observed about two or three in yours. You should each play one of the other's characters in an improvisational scene in which you discuss one of the following topics. Since this is largely to have you concentrate on "becoming" someone else, don't worry about having the scene reach a climax. Rather, treat this just as a discussion. To get started one of the characters can ask the other his opinion about one of the topics.

   a. Pornography;
   b. Teen pregnancy;
   c. Street gangs;
   d. The increasing crime rate;
   e. Conservation and ecology;
   f. The homeless.

At the end of two minutes, stop and the class will figure out the type of person you were portraying and some of his or her traits and mannerisms.

5. Have fun with this one. Use a character from your file, then add his or her traits to one of the following characters, who rushes to the center of town to see if other people know that this is the night the moon has just exploded.

   a. A young couple out on a date; they were sitting on a front porch, holding hands and looking up at the moon;
   b. An astronomer who has just been looking at the moon's craters;
   c. An astronaut;
   d. A hungry person waiting for all that green cheese to drop;
   e. The guy who was "the man in the moon" and who has come to earth to visit his family;
   f. The man in the moon's wife.

One by one or, as in the case of couples, two by two come to the town square until everyone is gathered. Simply show your reactions to each other and to the whole group. Decide if this is a serious situation or not

119

and what can be done about it.

Since there are so many people involved in this improvisation, make sure everyone has equal time in performing and speaking. The scene should take about four minutes.

6. Describe to the class five of the characters from your file. Now use one of them in an improvisational scene of two minutes in which the person is being interviewed for a particular job.

Choose a classmate to be the interviewer; then you will be an interviewer for that person. Before the interview begins, decide what the job will be. At the end of the scene, the interviewer will tell the person: 1) to come back for another interview; 2) that "I'm sorry, you don't fit our qualifications," or 3) the job is yours. This should be based on whether or not the interviewer thinks the character is suitable for the job.

At the end of the two minutes, you can, as yourself, tell the interviewer whether or not you think the character was a good candidate for the job. Then see if the class knows which of the five characters you played.

120

7. You are on an airplane that refuses to land. Here are some of the people on that plane. Split into groups of five or six and decide on who is going to play which character. Take three or four minutes to think about how you will react once the improvisation begins. Figure out who you are, that is, what you're like. Consider emotional and mental traits, as well as physical characteristics and mannerisms. In the playing space, if possible, arrange chairs in rows like you would find in an airplane. Leave a few feet for aisle space. You may get out of your seats during the improvisation if you like. But do remember that since you are on an airplane, you are somewhat restricted as to where you can go and what you can do.

Choose from among these characters:

a. The pilot;

b. A flight attendant;

c. A person flying for a job interview;

d. A person flying to his or her wedding;

e. An escaped criminal;

f. An elderly person who has never flown before;

g. A 12- or 13-year-old who is a brat;

h. A person who has an important business meeting;

i. A man and/or woman going to a daughter's college graduation;

j. A teenager running away from home.

8. If possible, arrange chairs two by two in the playing area. They represent seats on a ferris wheel that is stuck. Get together with someone else and choose one of the following pairs of characters:

a. A daredevil with a date who is nearly petrified with fear;

b. A husband and wife who have been talking about a divorce;

c. A child who has never before been on a carnival ride and a parent who didn't want to go on in the first place;

d. A frightened young woman and a young man who has a diamond ring he wants to give her;

121

e. A couple in their 80s who came to the carnival to try to recapture their youth and put some magic back into their relationship;

f. Two people in the military who have gone AWOL; they jumped on the ferris wheel to escape the military police who are after them.

Four of you can be on the ferris wheel at once. Do a three-minute improvisation.

9. These are solo improvisations. Think of a person who would logically do one of these activities and build a convincing character. Choose and combine traits of two characters from your file for this. You can have a day or two to plan this. Before you perform, read to the class the information you have about the two characters you combined. Try to make the activity as realistic or true to life as possible. The performance should last 60 to 90 seconds. Take a character doing one of the following:

a. Fishing and finally making a catch;

b. Trying to hail a taxi;

c. Feeding the pigeons in the park;

d. Exercising (any kind);

e. Playing golf;

f. Playing with a neighbor's dog or cat.

10. In this exercise, which should last about 90 seconds, you are to be yourself talking about a character. Build the talk around an object. The way you are to do this is to think of someone who would have owned it. It should be something that is unusual in some way, but which now is old or broken.

The idea is to build a whole character around the prop and make this character an interesting and likeable individual. You can say whatever you wish, except that you should answer these questions:

a. Why would the person have had this object?

b. How did the person feel about it, and why was it valuable to him or her?

c. Why does the person no longer have it?

11. Here is a variation of Exercise 10. Everyone should bring an object to school; it can be anything that once was useful or valuable but isn't any longer. All the objects should be placed at the front of the room. Each person gets to choose one of them. Then you have 10 minutes to plan a talk about the object, as a character who would logically value or use the item.

In the talk, tell why the object is important to you and its history — where you got it, how long you've had it, who owned it previously (if anyone did), how it lost its value (broken, outdated or whatever) and how you feel about that. Then say what the piece still means to you and if you plan to keep it or discard it.

12. Take a few days to work on this. Your character file may be very helpful here. What you have to do is cross the playing area six times. Each time you are to be a different age. Don't do a caricature of any age group; try to make the crosses as convincing and realistic as possible. Here are the ages you are to be:

a. 10 years old;

b. 20 years old;

c. 30 years old;

d. 50 years old;

e. 65 years old;

f. 90 years old.

13. Here's one that you should try to make funny. You are the crew of a spaceship, and one by one the five of you confess to what you forgot to bring with you that is very important to the mission.

Don't tell the others ahead of time what you've forgotten, but as a kind of insurance come up with two or three things in case someone else has selected the same thing.

If possible, arrange chairs in the playing area to simulate the inside of the ship. One by one, in any order that you wish, announce what you have forgotten. When each of the others announces what he or she has forgotten, react appropriately.

You all know that due to all this forgetfulness, you're going to have a tough time carrying out your mission, which is making maps, records, photographs and taking soil samples of the planet's surface.

The scene should last three or four minutes.

14. This exercise should test your concentration and imagination as well as your ability to come up with a good character.

Here are the openings of several stories. As a class, split into the odds and the evens.

The odds then should split into pairs; the evens should do the same thing.

a. This is what the odds are to do. Select one of the following stories and together decide where the story could logically go after taking into consideration the opening. You can have a week to plan out a scene that shows this. You can do it in outline form. If you wish, you can "draft" people from other groups to help you present the scene (but not plan it).

Based on the outline, present a four- to six-minute improvisation that shows how the story continues and ends.

b. Here now is what the evens do. Choose one of the endings the odds have presented. Disregard the written beginnings. Plan a scene that shows the beginning of what the odds have presented. But you cannot use the same beginning that already is here. You have to come up with something that logically could introduce the ending that the odds have chosen. You have a week also to plan this, and you are allowed to draft any of the odds to play characters. Good luck.

This is the beginning of a story called "White Noise."

The rain washed in gentle waves across the thick glass of the window. It was a comforting sound, conjuring up images of cozy fireplaces, braided rugs, a cat sleeping in front of the hearth.

Except the damn noise went on forever, Caleb thought, beating endlessly against the side of the cabin; filling even the desert till creek beds dry for years overflowed their banks.

It had sneaked up on everyone like an unpretentious summer shower. But it wasn't natural.

Caleb thought he'd better wake Pam and get them the hell out while they still could make it. They'd head straight up to the mountains, he thought.

He strode to the bedroom and laid a hand on Pam's shoulder. She opened her eyes, sleepily at first, then came instantly awake. It's worse, isn't it?" she asked.

"Much worse," Caleb answered. "You wouldn't believe how bad."

This is excerpted from a story called "White Christmas" by Scott Myrom. The central character is 16, and the story takes place in 1886.

Charley was a farmer's son, and he had the look of a farmer — six feet tall, lean and hard. But he dreamed of going to college and becoming a teacher. He loved the smell of books the way his father loved the smell of earth. Mary delighted in her son's thirst for learning, but Orrin couldn't think of a greater waste of time and money than college. He believed the land was the key to life, and working the land was the way of life. It was proper for a man to be able to read, write and cipher — he regretted his own illiteracy — but college was foolishness. He respected strength, courage and common sense; he didn't see that schooling produced any of these.

Though his beliefs were strong, Orrin didn't hold with strife under his own roof, so he kept his doubts to himself. But silence has its own eloquence. Charley sensed the lack of respect for his chosen course, and it hurt him deeply, for between father and son respect is as important as love itself.

* * *

Orrin had gone to the general store, and Charley was watching for him across the Nebraska prairie. In school, he had learned how the earth's roundness causes ships to appear bit by bit from beneath the horizon. Now his father's wagon heaved into sight like a clipper, yellow sails of dust billowing overhead. His father was lashing the horses furiously, the whip darting through the amber dust like black lightning.

Charley looked at the northern horizon and understood his father's urgency. A great, seething cloud was lifting ponderously over the edge of the world and rolling toward him like a prairie fire bleached white.

"Ma! Dad's coming, and there's a storm right behind him! A big one!" As Mary came out to look, the wagon clattered into the yard, and Orrin leaped out before it stopped moving. As he swung open the barn door, he yelled, "Everybody inside! I'm gonna move the cattle from the feedlot to the barn. I'll be in directly."

From the house, Charley and Mary saw Orrin run toward the feedlot. Then came a rushing sound, as if a train were flying by on seamless rails, and the storm washed over the farm like a tidal wave.

They waited. Night came quickly, and the world changed from white to black. "What about Dad?" said Charley. His voice sounded hollow in the freezing air.

"I don't know," said Mary. "When it hit, I thought I saw the barn door close. I don't know if it was your father or the wind."

"If he's in the barn, will he be safe?"

"Maybe . . . I can't say. We'll just have to wait till it's over."

"Maybe we won't have to wait," said Charley. "I've got an idea."

This is excerpted from a short story called "The Vow."

He was a prodigy; that's the only apt word. He cared about little other than the piano. The trouble was his parents didn't start him on lessons until he was 14, and he felt he had a lot of catching up to do. So his teacher set him a course of lessons that was supposed to end four years hence when he graduated from high school. He finished the four years in less than six months.

I never understood; there was always a piano in his home, and suddenly with no previous indication of interest, he developed this need, this passion that nothing but Chopin could satisfy.

Every weekday for four hours after school he sat at the piano. Every weekend and holiday he sat there eight hours until his parents told him he had to do something else.

Knowing he was capable of such passion, maybe it shouldn't have surprised me how he fell for Dolly whom he met on the city bus one Friday afternoon on the way home from his lesson.

He was 16 or nearly so, and it was love at first sight. He told me later he saw her, doffed his hat like an old country gentleman, and took the only available seat in the bus, of course, beside her.

Dolly was more than two years older. He was a high school junior, she a sophomore at the University of Pittsburgh. She smiled.

The name of this short story is "When Benny Came to Town."

Nobody could say why Benny came to town or why he stayed. Some said it was simply because his old Hudson had broken down in front of Chapello's Garage, and he hadn't enough money to fix it, so he sold it to Vic Chapello and took a room at the hotel.

Some of the folks didn't like it — that Bob Miller's wife Ruby had rented him that room. Benny was a black man, one of the few ever to come to Rock Creek, Pennsylvania, and the first ever to stay.

It was the 40s and few in town had ever met a black man before. Most of the town didn't hate him; some did. Brody Thompson was maybe the worst.

Brody and I were seniors in high school, both in marching band. It was a bright fall day, fresh smelling, like the seasons had gotten mixed up somehow and were heading into summer instead of winter. We were practicing out on the ball field the last period of the day.

At the end of the routine we're facing front toward the bleachers and further on the Restful Arms Hotel, when Brody sidesteps a little and jabs me in the ribs with the sliding part of his trombone.

"Hey, Brody, what the hell —" I started to say, but he's nodding his head toward the other side of the street, and what do I see but this old black guy out in front of the hotel clipping the rose bushes.

"It's that nigger," Brody said.

And that made me mad. I don't even know why it made me mad. But every time I heard that word it created a kind of whirlwind deep inside that stirred up my gut.

"Negro," I said. "You mean Negro, don't you?"

Brody hisses at me through his teeth. "Ssssss," like a damn snake. "Ssssss," he says. "He's a nigger."

I decided to drop it for then. I mean I didn't even know old Benny. So I just looked long and hard at Brody . . .

Later, as we were walking back toward the school,

Brody kept crowding me out toward the road across from the Restful Arms, a green shingled building like all the other houses in town, only two or three times as big.

"What the hell are you doing, Brody?" I asked, bumping him back.

"I want to get a closer look. I ain't never seen one of them things up close before."

I looked at him but didn't answer.

"What the hell is it with you, Mike?" Brody asked. "You in love with that old man or something?"

"No, I'm not in love with him," I said, and I felt myself getting really angry.

"You could have fooled me."

15. A good source for ideas is the newspaper. Often you can learn about interesting people in feature stories or even unusual people and events in the news stories. For this exercise, go through a recent newspaper and find either a news or feature story that interests you.

The class will break into groups of four to six. Read your story to your group and brainstorm for 10 minutes on how the person from the newspaper can become the basis of an improvisation involving your group.

After you have brainstormed on each item brought to your group, decide which idea you think will work best. Then work out the details of a four- to six-minute improvisation which you will present some time over the next few days.

16. The photo on page 130 was taken about the turn of the century.

Get together with three classmates and write a character description of these two people, including what you think they're like. Put yourself in their places and figure out what sorts of problems they might have at this period of time and who else might be involved. Do try to make this something realistic — although, if you wish, it can be humorous. But considering that these were real people, treat them with respect.

Then decide on who is going to play which roles and do a four-to six-minute improvisation with the two people in the photo as the central characters and two others as the supporting cast, somehow involved in whatever problem it is the people are having.

Part IV:

EXERCISES FOR CHARACTERS, SCENES AND PLAYS

Working With Existing Characters and Scenes

In ways it is easier to work with characters who already exist because much of the work is already done for you.

For instance, you learn a great deal about the character of Swedey in this excerpt from "The Camp Robber" by Herbert M. Kulman. The story takes place in 1894.

> Swedey had been about as close to pure whiteness as anybody could get without being an albino, especially as he had gotten older and his blond hair gave way to baldness. When he was clean, the only color he had was the clear blue of his small piggy eyes and the tobacco stains on his teeth. He came from the old country as a boy, working in the lumber camps in Minnesota and then moved to the West when the big timber of the Great Lakes was gone. He lived a hard life and avenged each pain and disappointment until it was habit and finally need. Cookie, the halfbreed belly robber, claimed to see him pull the tail off a live mouse. Many men knew, without even seeing him do it, that he nicked their axe blades, cheated at cards . . . But a logger he was — a logger who could fell trees "on a liberty dime if you dared 'im," could lift logs, could whip horses into "pullin' loads they can't," could boast like Bunyan and then do it most of the time, sneering a, "let's see you try it."
>
> As Jack Gortner would often say, "Nobody seems to know just how Swedey got so mean. Some say he got that way from being weaned on a goat, but I wouldn't blame a goat. He was mean just because he was."

In a story the author often can write descriptions of the character, as Kulman did with Swedey. In a play, it's usually only the lines and maybe a brief description that gives you clues to what a character is like. Still you need to understand the character to play the person well.

1. This is a two-part exercise.

a. Work with a partner in writing a two-minute scene

in which Swedey talks with someone else. It should be the sort of character he'd know or be likely to meet, such as another logger. Read the scene to the rest of the class, who should discuss whether or not they thought you were true to Swedey's character and why.

b. Choose a two-character scene of about two minutes from one of the play excerpts in the book and read it over a few times, but don't memorize the lines. Now, with a partner, write a short outline of the scene and go over it until you have it in mind. Using just the outline, present the scene with improvised dialog. Have someone tape what you do so you can see how you changed the lines. Have the class discuss whether or not your characters were believable and consistent with the existing characters.

In ways, it's harder to work with established characters because you have less freedom. You can't disregard any part of the character that's already established. You can only add on to it.

Here is a play written by Betty J. Reeves.

MARKET

SETTING: The action occurs in a small neighborhood market with three checkout stands, four aisles of double-sided shelves, meat counter, produce area, and frozen food section. Alongside the glass "Entrance" and "Exit" doors are a row of grocery carts and a refrigerated liquor case.

AT RISE: VELDA, a thin woman in her early 40s, is diligently cleaning the counters of the checkout stands. JIMMY, 16-year-old bagger, enters from the "Employees Only" door in the rear.

VELDA: It's about time.

(JIMMY reaches under a counter and pulls out his store jacket. VELDA looks in disgust at the stains and wrinkles as he pulls it on.)

VELDA: *(Handing him keys)* **Open up and stock the bins.**

JIMMY: *(He goes to door, unlocks it, then throws his arm*

134

against his forehead as though shielding his eyes from a blinding light and staggers back.) **Agghh ...**

VELDA: **You're sick, you know that?** *(She switches on a register, which immediately begins beeping and flashing.)* **You been foolin' around with my machine?**

JIMMY: *(Imitating a Michael Jackson routine, he dances back to VELDA.)* **Would Jim here be foolin' with a terminal retoolin'? Would I neuter your computer?**

VELDA: **I asked you a civil question. Don't give me that goofy talk.**

(BOY and GIRL, in their early teens, enter, followed by OLD MAN and OLD WOMAN.)

JIMMY: *(Watching GIRL and BOY, hand in hand, walk by)* **Oooh ...** *(He puts his hands underneath his shirt and mocks a pounding heart.)* **You're so sweet.** *(He puckers up his lips and kisses the air.)*

VELDA: **Stop it.** *(She jabs JIMMY in the ribs with her elbow. Then to OLD MAN and OLD WOMAN)* **Hello. How are you today?**

OLD MAN: **Howdy.**

OLD WOMAN: **Good morning.**

OLD MAN: **We're moving a little slow. Had the family over last night. Our two great-grandbabies.**

VELDA: **That's nice.**

OLD MAN: **Yep. Everybody's doin' fine.**

OLD WOMAN: **Wore me out.**

OLD MAN: *(Nodding his head to OLD WOMAN)* **The wife here has to run around, do everything. Can't sit still a minute.**

OLD WOMAN: **Well, of course, you've got to do for your kids.** *(To VELDA)* **Isn't that right?**

VELDA: **Sure is.**

(OLD MAN and OLD WOMAN head toward the shopping carts, while the BOY and GIRL go directly to the candy section. OLD MAN wistfully watching the BOY and GIRL, stands idly by as the OLD WOMAN checks over the merits

of each cart.)

OLD WOMAN: Getting so you can't find a decent cart anymore. If they're not all sticky, then the wheels go every which way. *(To OLD MAN)* Well, don't just stand there.

OLD MAN: Any one of them looks fine to me.

OLD WOMAN: I guess you thought that boy at the checkout looked fine too.

OLD MAN: Course. *(He smiles at JIMMY.)*

OLD WOMAN: Take a look at his hair.

OLD MAN: What?

OLD WOMAN: Plastered down all over his head. He looks like something out of a cellar.

OLD MAN: A cellar?

OLD WOMAN: You know what I mean. Like in the movies. *(OLD MAN laughs and shakes his head.)* I'm talking about vampires.

OLD MAN: Ain't no such thing.

OLD WOMAN: Of course there's no such thing as vampires. I know that. What I'm saying is that kids nowadays want to be weird.

OLD MAN: I don't believe that. *(He points to BOY and GIRL at candy shelves.)* Looky there. At those two kids.

OLD WOMAN: *(She turns and looks at BOY and GIRL, then turns back to cart.)* They're just darling.

OLD MAN: See how polite he is.

OLD WOMAN: Regular Sir Galahad.

OLD MAN: Bet she's his first girl.

(JOGGER enters, trots over to liquor shelves, and grabs a six-pack. Running in place, he pays VELDA and exits. JIMMY assumes "Rocky" stance and VELDA shakes her head and starts sorting and restacking magazine racks.)

OLD WOMAN: What're you mumbling about? Got to stop that. You're starting to sound like some old bum, going around mumbling.

OLD MAN: *(Speaking louder)* I say she's his girlfriend

and that's real cute.

(OLD MAN and OLD WOMAN move toward meat case. OLD WOMAN browses among the meat while OLD MAN watches BOY and GIRL. OLD WOMAN selects a package of meat and looks around for OLD MAN and cart. OLD MAN is still watching BOY and GIRL.)

OLD WOMAN: **Want some pork chops tomorrow?** *(Looks at OLD MAN, but he doesn't answer.)* **I know you hear me.** *(She puts her hands on her hips and calls out to OLD MAN.)* **You just don't listen to me.**

OLD MAN: *(Looking at her)* **Do what?**

OLD WOMAN: **Pork chops. Tomorrow?**

OLD MAN: **Why sure. That'd be nice.**

OLD WOMAN: **Well, push that thing down here then. I'm not going to carry all this stuff myself.** *(OLD MAN rolls the cart up to meat case and OLD WOMAN carefully arranges her purchases.)*

OLD MAN: **I remember my first time . . . my first girl. Yeah, I must have been all of fifteen years old.**

OLD WOMAN: **Who's fifteen?**

OLD MAN: **I was.**

OLD WOMAN: **Well, that's a long time ago.**

OLD MAN: **Time don't mean nothin' when it comes to some things.**

OLD WOMAN: **You can't recall what you had for breakfast this morning, and you're telling me you know what you did sixty years ago?** *(She pulls out a piece of paper, her grocery list, and peers at the items on it.)* **You're crazy. Now let me alone so I can figure out what I need.**

OLD MAN: **She was a pretty little thing.**

OLD WOMAN: *(Walking ahead of him)* **Come on. We haven't got all day.**

OLD MAN: **Yellow hair, and a black ribbon she wore.** *(He stops the cart in the middle of the aisle.)* **Wide it was, and black. Black velvet.**

137

(The OLD MAN and OLD WOMAN continue, stopping near the BOY and GIRL while the OLD WOMAN selects a bag of gumdrops and the OLD man watches the two young people. OLD MAN and OLD WOMAN pass BOY and GIRL and turn into next aisle.)

OLD WOMAN: **Can't understand a word you're saying. You've got to speak up if you want a person to hear you.**

OLD MAN: *(Raising his voice)* **My first girl, I'm talking about my first girlfriend.** *(He places his hand on his wife's arm, stopping her.)* **Like those two. I never told you.** *(BOY and GIRL take their purchases to checkout stand and exit.)*

OLD WOMAN: *(Turning away from him, she surveys the brightly lighted store.)* **You told me about her. You don't remember things right, you know that?** *(She starts walking down the aisle.)*

OLD MAN: **Sure, I do. I remember. Her name was Angela. I called her Angie. And she was a little thing.** *(He holds his hand level with his chin.)* **Shorter'n me. I really liked that. I was the shortest guy in class.**

OLD WOMAN: *(Back to peering at her list)* **You were a shrimp all right. You still are.** *(Pointing to cart)* **Push the cart.**

OLD MAN: **OK, OK.** *(Her pushes the cart to the end of the aisle and follows his wife to the dairy case.)*

OLD WOMAN: **We need some oleo.**

OLD MAN: **I ever tell you about Angie?**

OLD WOMAN: *(Looking at dairy items)* **Look at that. No Blue Cow. I swear, you get to like something and they take it off the shelves.** *(She rummages among the shelves.)*

OLD MAN: **I said ...**

OLD WOMAN: **Not here.** *(To OLD MAN)* **Call that stock boy and see if they have some in the back.**

OLD MAN: *(Bending and pointing)* **How about that kind?**

We never tried that.

OLD WOMAN: That kind is pure butter. Bad for you. Besides, it costs too much. Go on, call that boy.

OLD MAN: *(Looking over at JIMMY, who is pasting up new sign on the wall behind checkstand)* He's busy. *(Grinning to himself)* Anyway, you sure you want him to come over? Nobody here but us. He might get hungry, take a bite out of your neck, and . . .

OLD WOMAN: *(Laughing)* I swear, you're a crazy old coot, you are. Now go on, call him over.

OLD MAN: *(Walking over to JIMMY)* Think you could help us, son?

JIMMY: *(Following OLD MAN)* Sure. Whatcha need?

OLD WOMAN: You got any Blue Cow oleo in the back?

JIMMY: We don't carry that. Sorry. *(He returns to checkout. To VELDA)* Now they want to buy something I never heard of. Probably hasn't been on the market since the Civil War. *(Grabbing a poster and some tape)* I hope I never get like that.

VELDA: What?

JIMMY: Where all I got to do is worry about what kind of grease I smear on my bread.

OLD MAN: I was saying did I ever tell you about Angie?

OLD WOMAN: I heard. *(Dumping several items into the cart)* I just don't know why you have to bring up things from back then.

OLD MAN: It's nice to remember. *(He stops and stares into space.)* Nice to remember happy times, like the first girl you had a crush on.

OLD WOMAN: That's all over, all over and done with. She's probably dead by now. It doesn't matter anyway. *(She pulls at his sleeve.)* We've got shopping to do.

OLD MAN: But I like to think about the happy times.

OLD WOMAN: Happy times.

OLD MAN: Times you felt good. Don't matter when they happened.

OLD WOMAN: Is that so?

OLD MAN: Sure.

OLD WOMAN: Then remember them right. Face the truth. Don't make up stories. *(The OLD MAN pushes the cart close to the OLD WOMAN and looks at her.)*

OLD MAN: What do you mean?

OLD WOMAN: That girl, that *(Pause)* Angie.

OLD MAN: What about her?

OLD WOMAN: You told me. Her dad had the tobacco shop down on Olive Street, right?

OLD MAN: That's right, yeah, that's right. And a nice little place. She used to help out Saturdays.

OLD WOMAN: You worked Saturdays, too.

OLD MAN: I sure did. *(Leaning on the cart)* Worked after school and Saturdays.

OLD WOMAN: She never used to come in at all until she found out you were working.

OLD MAN: That's right. She never did come down till I started workin'.

OLD WOMAN: And then she came down every Saturday.

OLD MAN: She'd sit on this stool by the door, the door to the alley. And she'd smile at me when I carried out the trash.

OLD WOMAN: She did more than smile.

OLD MAN: Yeah. She used to open the door for me.

OLD WOMAN: She opened more than that.

OLD MAN: What?

OLD WOMAN: And she had these teeth.

OLD MAN: *(Straightening up and looking around at the shelves)* I don't know what you're talkin' about.

OLD WOMAN: Sure, you do. She was little and cute and she liked you, but when she smiled, she had these awful teeth. *(Baring her teeth)* Like this.

OLD MAN: She couldn't help it. They couldn't fix buck-teeth back then.

OLD WOMAN: And she used to follow you out to the alley,

140

to the ashpit where you dumped the trash. *(The OLD MAN tries to push the cart, to move on, but the OLD WOMAN grips the cart and stops him.)*

OLD MAN: I don't remember.

OLD WOMAN: Of course you don't. You don't want to remember the truth.

OLD MAN: *(He tries to move the cart.)* **C'mon, c'mon, woman. What else you got on that list?**

OLD WOMAN: Never mind the list. You want to talk about happy times. *(She crumples the list and shoves it in her pocket.)* All right, let's talk about those happy times with Angie. She used to follow you out, tell you how strong you were to carry all those big boxes. *(Into the story now, she mimics a young girl's adoring manner.)*

OLD MAN: She was nice, a nice girl.

OLD WOMAN: Sure she was, real nice. So nice she used to let you —

OLD MAN: Aw, we was just . . .

OLD WOMAN: And you. You were so sweet that when she asked you to kiss her, you took one look at those teeth and ran off. Nice kid you were, real nice.
(During the OLD WOMAN's last speech, the OLD MAN has covered his ears. When she finishes, his hands drop to his sides and he stands, very still, in the middle of the aisle.)

OLD WOMAN: There you go, getting me all upset again. *(She pulls her list out of her pocket and smooths it out.)* You and your happy memories. *(She studies her list carefully, moving her lips soundlessly over the items, then glances around at the shelves.)* Don't need any of this. We've already been here. *(She looks at the OLD MAN who stands motionless, staring at the floor.)* Let's get you some of your sherbet, you're almost out. *(She reaches over and pulls the edges of his sweater together.)* Better button up now, it's cold over by the frozen stuff. *(Slowly, the OLD MAN begins to fasten his sweater. OLD*

WOMAN *pushes the cart down the aisle toward the frozen
food section.)* **Better get a move on.** *(The OLD MAN
looks up and sees his wife walking away from him.)*

OLD MAN: Hold on, woman. *(He follows her.)* **You know
something? I never told you, but I got that little gal
a present once. Candy. Orange jelly slices. All sugar
on the outside, and big as real oranges. You remember the kind.** *(OLD WOMAN slows down and
waits.)* **Some guys never bought their girls nothin',
but I did.** *(The OLD MAN catches up to OLD WOMAN.)*
**Cost me too. Back in those days I didn't have
much** . . . *(They turn the corner as the curtain falls.)*

Directors often have the actors improvise scenes before they
have the lines memorized. This can help in at least three ways.

a) It can give the actors confidence. They see that although
they may not know the lines exactly, they know the sense of the
play.

b) When actors are forced to concentrate on characters in
order to improvise what would be logical for them to say, the
actors most often learn to know the characters better.

c) Only a tiny bit of the character's entire life is shown
on-stage during a performance. The director may want the actors
to improvise scenes not related to the play so their characters
become real to them.

Of course, the actors should have studied the script so that
they understand the characters, the action and the message.

2. Read through "Market" a couple of times to make sure
you understand what Reeves means it to convey. Figure out what
the characters are like as individuals and their relationships to
each other.

Here are some questions you might want to discuss.

a. What is the play's theme? All plays have a theme
or message. This is usually tied in with the author's
views on life. The theme is what the author wants
to say to an audience. It might be something playful
or something serious. For instance, in Thornton

Wilder's play *Our Town*, the theme is that we should all pay attention to others, to really be aware of them before it's too late.

Obviously, the message in "Market" is not light or playful. The author is saying something serious about life and relationships. What do you think this is? Why do you think so? Point to parts of the play that show this specifically.

b. What is the relationship between the Old Man and the Old Woman? How do they feel about each other?

c. Why do you suppose the Old Man keeps thinking about his first girlfriend? How does the Old Woman feel about this?

d. What attitudes can you detect that the Old Man and Old Woman have about each other? Pick out lines in the script that show this.

e. How do you feel about them? Are they likeable or not?

f. Is the Old Woman justified in what she does?

g. What effect do the Old Woman's words have on the Old Man? Pick the parts of the script that show this? What exactly is she saying to him when she says his memories aren't right? How do you know this?

h. What sort of person is Jimmy? Do you like him? Why? Why do you suppose he "puts down" everyone who comes into the store?

i. Why do you think the playwright included a character such as Jimmy?

j. What sort of person is Velda? Do you like her? Why?

k. How do Jimmy and Velda feel about each other? Point to lines in the script that show this feeling.

l. The character of the Boy and Girl are not nearly as fully developed as the characters of the Old Man and the Old Woman, nor even so much as those of Jimmy and Velda. What purpose do they serve in the script? Why did the playwright include them? Can you point to any lines that show what they are like? What is their relationship with each other? Why do you suppose they have no interaction with the other characters?

    m. Why is the jogger included? What part does he play in the overall unfolding of the script? Do you think he is a necessary character? Why or why not?

    n. As you learned earlier, most plays have conflict that builds to a turning point and climax. What conflict occurs in this play? Do you think it builds effectively? Where do the turning point and climax occur? Do you think the resolution is satisfactory? Why?

    o. Raise any other questions you have about the script.

    3. Split into groups of six. Each of you should choose the character you would like to play in "Market" (exclusive of the jogger). Then working as a group, come up with a one- to two-page outline covering all the important points or developments in the script. Take a day or two to make sure you have the outline in mind. Then without trying to learn the lines, present the play from this outline, improvising the lines and portraying the characters as you think the author intended them to be played.

Keep in mind that it's okay to view a character a little differently from the way anyone else does. Just make sure your interpretation is consistent with what the playwright has written. You can add whatever you like to the character, just so it doesn't destroy any part that already exists.

Your improvisation should take anywhere from six to 10 minutes. If there aren't enough people or it doesn't work out to have six to a group, you can eliminate the BOY and the GIRL.

ANALYZING YOUR CHARACTERS

Whether or not you are working with an existing character, there are a number of questions you should try to answer to make your character convincing. With an established character, some of the answers will be in the script. But there are always things the playwright has not included that you might want to know to make the character realistic.

Think of a character as being like an iceberg. A large part is buried below the surface, but there is a depth from which to draw.

The things it helps to know are 1) physical characteristics,

2) background, 3) attitudes and beliefs, 4) and patterns of behavior.

Physical characteristics you might want to know include things the character has some control over. So you might try to answer such questions as:

- What is the character's taste in clothes?
- How does he or she wear her hair?
- What sort of jewelry does the character wear?

Of course, other things influence a character's tastes in clothing and hair style. As you know, people who are more extroverted often wear "louder" clothes, things that call attention to themselves. Most often an introvert wouldn't wear this sort of thing. So even if you have no choice of what you wear in a play or improvisation, consider what your costume says about the personality of the character you're portraying.

These are some questions you can ask about the character's background:

- Where did he or she grow up?
- Was the family rich or poor? How did this affect the character's outlook?
- Is the character well-educated, or did the person drop out of school?
- What are the person's interests? Hobbies?
- What sort of job does the person have? How does he or she feel about this?
- What about speech patterns? Is there an accent? Does the person use a lot of slang? Why? Does the person's job, education or area of the country (now or growing up) have a bearing on the way he or she talks? How does the speech portray personality?
- Is the character well liked? By the other characters in a play? By family and friends? Does he or she have generally positive relationships with others?
- What are the biggest influences on the person's life?
- Is the character pessimistic or optimistic; introverted or extroverted?

Of course, all the things are interrelated. A person's background can have an affect on how he or she dresses and on relationships with other people.

What about attitudes and beliefs?

- What are the character's political and religious beliefs?
- Are they generally strict or lenient?
- What are their goals?

What are the character's behavior patterns?

- Does the person work hard?
- Does he or she take time to enjoy life?
- Is the character nervous or relaxed; normal or neurotic?
- Does the person follow an unvarying schedule, or is the behavior more varied or even erratic?

These are just a sample of the kinds of questions you can ask to learn about the character. You can try to figure out anything that will make him or her more realistic for you or for the audience. Knowing the answers can make you feel more confident.

Following is the script of "Vampire," which has only two characters, Gordonov and Jeannie.

VAMPIRE

SETTING: The action occurs in the kitchen of JEANNIE's apartment in a middle-class neighborhood in San Diego. There are a table and four chairs center. Up Left a coffee maker sits on a counter. There is a door right.

AT RISE: As the scene opens, JEANNIE and GORDONOV are sitting at the table drinking coffee.

JEANNIE: I appreciate your walking me home.

GORDONOV: But something's bothering you.

JEANNIE: I don't know how to say this.

GORDONOV: You sound so serious.

JEANNIE: I'm fond of you.

GORDONOV: Surely, you've guessed how I feel about you.

JEANNIE: Maybe you'd better tell me, Jack.

GORDONOV: I've never felt this way about anyone else.

146

I never really expected to. After all these years of my life.

JEANNIE: *(Laughing)* You make yourself sound ancient.

GORDONOV: Maybe I am.

JEANNIE: Oh, Jack, I'm so frightened. *(She stands, crosses to the coffee maker and turns it off.)*

GORDONOV: *(Rushing to her, spinning her around)* Why? I wouldn't want to frighten you. I'd never mean to frighten you. *(JEANNIE crosses back to the table. GORDONOV follows.)*

JEANNIE: *(Turning to GORDONOV, she raises his hand to her lips, kissing his knuckles.)* I never meant to feel this way about anyone ever again. That's what I mean. That's what frightens me. *(She crosses to her chair and sits.)*

GORDONOV: I think I've loved you from the first moment your uncle introduced us.

JEANNIE: Have you?

GORDONOV: You know I have. How could you help but know?

JEANNIE: Yes. *(She smiles sadly.)* And despite how I felt about you, I held back.

GORDONOV: From your point of view, I suppose I have acted strangely.

JEANNIE: *(Shrugs.)* We've been seeing each other for — what? — six months. I know absolutely nothing about you.

GORDONOV: What would you like to know?

JEANNIE: Well, for starters, where are you from?

GORDONOV: I was born in Europe. I'm not sure exactly where. *(JEANNIE looks at him strangely and frowns.)* My mother said I was born in the Ukraine. But I don't remember living there. I remember the lights of Paris, the Cathedral of Notre Dame. And the Black Forest. I remember that. And South Africa and Spain and Scandinavia.

JEANNIE: Is that so?

GORDONOV: Yes, but — but I have to tell you something.

JEANNIE: What is it?

GORDONOV: *(Shakes his head.)* I — I don't know if I should tell you or not. You won't believe me.

JEANNIE: Try me.

GORDONOV: *(Pause)* I'm a vampire.

JEANNIE: A vampire. Really?

GORDONOV: You probably think I'm crazy.

JEANNIE: I didn't say that.

GORDONOV: I've lived in a hundred places, Jeannie. I've had a score of careers. Still, in most ways I'm just like you.

JEANNIE: *(Pulling a sweater from the back of the chair and slipping it around her shoulders)* Just like me?

GORDONOV: Would it help to say I'd do anything to be just like you. *(Pause)* I never thought I'd say that. I vowed I'd never become involved with anyone ever again. I've had too many disappointments. Too many friends have died.

JEANNIE: I never told you about Peter, did I?

GORDONOV: *(Puzzled)* No.

JEANNIE: We were in love. He was a computer expert. One day something went wrong with a computer at a bank in Solana Beach. No one else knew what to do, so they called him to come in. He was hurrying to get there; it was three-thirty in the morning, the freeways covered in fog. *(Shakes her head.)* His car ran off the road — *(She begins to cry.)*

GORDONOV: Oh, Jeannie, I'm sorry.

JEANNIE: We were in love, talking about marriage. Yet we came from totally different backgrounds. *(She looks into GORDONOV's eyes.)* I don't know ... if the marriage would have worked.

GORDONOV: I'm sorry.

148

JEANNIE: So for a lot of reasons I thought I'd never fall in love again. And now I have.

GORDONOV: I have an idea. *(Glancing at his watch)* I'll show you where I live.

JEANNIE: Where you live?

GORDONOV: Yes. A three-room house. A cottage. With a waterbed. I don't sleep in a coffin. And I don't sleep all day. I do a lot of work at night. Only because it's cooler then and quiet. I write historical novels. Why not? I've lived in the times I write about. *(Pause)* I sleep till ten or ten-thirty and then get up. The daylight doesn't harm me.

JEANNIE: You still insist that everything you're telling me is true?

GORDONOV: Oh, yes, it's true. Ask your Uncle Don. He knows.

JEANNIE: He does?

GORDONOV: I got careless, flying in the light of the moon.

JEANNIE: Jack ...

GORDONOV: Please, Jeannie. Just listen. *(JEANNIE shrugs.)* That night we met?

JEANNIE: What about it?

GORDONOV: I'd just met your uncle too.

JEANNIE: Really?

GORDONOV: He saw me landing on the roof. The roof of Thrifty Drug Store. He'd come to pick you up after work at the card shop.

JEANNIE: Listen, Jack, I don't —

GORDONOV: You said you love me.

JEANNIE: Yes, I did.

GORDONOV: Then give me one chance.

JEANNIE: I have so many doubts.

GORDONOV: Look, Jeannie, will you step outside with me? Out on the porch.

JEANNIE: I don't understand.

149

GORDONOV: If you only could know how it's been. All those years alone. Losing the friends I'd made in the early years. Watching them die. Watching their children die. Their grandchildren. Their great-grandchildren.

JEANNIE: *(With a look of compassion)* Now it's my turn to be sorry. You said you wanted to step outside.

GORDONOV: Yes.

JEANNIE: *(Standing)* All right, then, let's go.

GORDONOV: *(Having second thoughts)* I'm not sure we should do this. I was going to —

JEANNIE: What were you going to do?

GORDONOV: I was going to — I think I've changed my mind.

JEANNIE: *(Laughing)* What were you going to do? Turn yourself into a bat?

GORDONOV: That's exactly what I was going to do.

JEANNIE: This has gone far enough.

GORDONOV: *(Hurt)* Maybe it has.

JEANNIE: *(Softening)* I'm sorry. I don't mean that the way it sounds. All right. Let's go outside.

GORDONOV: Are you sure?

JEANNIE: Come on, Jack, let's go.

GORDONOV: Against my better judgment.

JEANNIE: I thought you wanted —

GORDONOV: I wanted so much for you to believe me, to trust me, to know I'd never lie to you.

JEANNIE: *(Reaching out to him then drawing back)* I know you wouldn't lie.

GORDONOV: What do you mean? Do you think I'm deluding myself?

JEANNIE: I don't think you're deluding yourself. But I have to be sure —

GORDONOV: You think I belong in a straightjacket.

JEANNIE: I —

GORDONOV: All right. I'll do it then.

JEANNIE: Do it?

GORDONOV: You said you'd step outside. *(JEANNIE shrugs.)*

GORDONOV: Let's go. *(He takes her by the elbow and leads her Off Right.)*

JEANNIE: *(As she exits)* If this is what it takes ... *(For a moment the stage is empty. Then suddenly, JEANNIE cries out. In a moment she enters, crosses to a chair and sits. GORDONOV comes in a few seconds later.)*

JEANNIE: All right, Jack. OK. I believe you.

GORDONOV: I'm still the same person. The same person who loves you.

JEANNIE: But you're *not* just a man. You're a —

GORDONOV: A monster? Go ahead and say it.

JEANNIE: No, Jack! That isn't what I meant.

GORDONOV: *(Leaning on the back of a chair)* I was wrong. I knew it. I knew it was the wrong thing to do. I thought maybe if you understood.

JEANNIE: All those things you told me are true?

GORDONOV: All those things?

JEANNIE: About ... about daylight not hurting you. About loving me?

GORDONOV: Of course, they're true.

JEANNIE: But you're a vampire.

GORDONOV: *(Shaking his head and smiling tentatively)* I can't deny it. Especially now.

JEANNIE: How many — I mean — I never knew there were —

GORDONOV: *(Sighing)* I really don't know much more about it than you do. *(Pulling out the chair)* May I sit down?

JEANNIE: *(A pause, and then she shrugs.)* You can sit down.

GORDONOV: *(He sits, hands folded on the table.)* I'm — so far as I know — I'm the last of my kind.

JEANNIE: There's no one else like you?

GORDONOV: No one. I've looked for years.

JEANNIE: How lonely! How terribly, terribly lonely you must be. You must have been.

GORDONOV: Thanks, Jeannie. At least, thanks for that.

JEANNIE: I think I must be crazy, Jack. I really must be crazy.

GORDONOV: To have fallen in love with me? To . . . love me still.

JEANNIE: To have doubted you. Even a little.

GORDONOV: *(Reaching his hands across the table)* I'm me. I'm still me.

JEANNIE: How did — how did you become —?

GORDONOV: I don't know. My mother was . . . my mother was a vampire.

JEANNIE: Your mother?

GORDONOV: She died so many years ago.

JEANNIE: *(Upset)* But I thought —

GORDONOV: We lived forever?

JEANNIE: Yes.

GORDONOV: Maybe we do. Maybe my mother . . . didn't want to live . . . anymore. I've felt that way.

JEANNIE: *(Taking his hands)* Oh, Jack.

GORDONOV: After my mother died, way back at the end of the seventeenth century, I had no one. And that was best. When I made friends, they died. But I continued to live. Do you understand? I can't bear to lose more friends.

JEANNIE: I understand. But is there nothing you can do?

GORDONOV: Do?

JEANNIE: I suppose not. No matter how much you want them to live, you can't realistically do anything about it. Except turn them into vampires. Then their lives are just as lonely —

GORDONOV: You do understand, don't you? At least a little. As much as a mortal —

JEANNIE: I love you. Nothing else matters.

GORDONOV: If I were mortal ... every hour, every moment of my life would be precious. I couldn't bear to lose you. If we could be together —

JEANNIE: You'd want to be mortal? You'd wish for a death sentence?

GORDONOV: *(Standing)* If we could be together. *(He walks behind her chair, leans down and kisses the top of her head.)* Look, Jeannie, all I have left of my mother is this. *(He takes a chain from around his neck, a fine gold chain with a cross and hands it to JEANNIE.)* Are you surprised?

JEANNIE: Surprised?

GORDONOV: Don't you know the legends? That vampires are the antithesis of all that is holy. That we're evil personified.

JEANNIE: I suppose I've heard those stories.

GORDONOV: If they were true, would I have this cross? A cross given me by my mother when — I called him father. But I knew him so briefly. And within a few decades he and my mother were dead.

JEANNIE: *(Her voice filled with compassion)* I'm so sorry.

GORDONOV: Mother never explained to me where I'd come from, how I'd been created. For years I hounded libraries, reading texts in a score of languages. What I learned was never worthwhile. Based on misconceptions, mistaken ideas.

JEANNIE: You don't know how you became a vampire?

GORDONOV: So far as I know, I've always been.

JEANNIE: I thought — I thought vampires couldn't have children.

GORDONOV: I can't answer that. I just don't know.

JEANNIE: But if you were always a vampire, that means you must have been one as a child.

GORDONOV: I age, Jeannie. It takes hundreds of years to become mature. But I have changed from boy to

153

adolescent to young man. So maybe I'm not immor-
tal.

JEANNIE: You said your mother died.

GORDONOV: Long before she should have, I believe.

JEANNIE: To have had a mother and then — How did
it happen?

GORDONOV: Jeannie, among the many legends about
us, there's one that says a vampire can create other
vampires by biting their necks.

JEANNIE: Create others?

GORDONOV: Oh, no! Don't think I'd change you. I
wouldn't. Not for anything. I wouldn't allow you to
see everything you hold dear crumble to dust and
fade away. It's the opposite. To limit my own life.
(Pause) I think I know what my mother did. When I
was self-sufficient. Able to be on my own.

JEANNIE: Jack?

GORDONOV: Have you ever pricked your finger, stuck
it into your mouth and sucked the wound?

JEANNIE: *(Bewildered)* Everyone has, I suppose.

GORDONOV: And you do love me? You still love me?

JEANNIE: *(Nods.)* You know the answer to that.

GORDONOV: If I can turn you into a vampire by biting
your neck — *(He shrugs.)* Doesn't it stand to reason
that the opposite would work?

JEANNIE: I could — You'd become a human being?

GORDONOV: It's worth a try. Isn't it? *(Releasing a sigh)*
All right, here's what we'll do. Just what my mother
did, I think. A small cut, no more. *(He walks to the
counter and picks up a knife.)* Like this. *(He runs the
blade of the knife across his finger.)*

JEANNIE: I don't understand.

GORDONOV: I'll blot away the blood.

*(GORDONOV wipes his fingers on a paper napkin. He
holds out his hand, takes JEANNIE's hand and kisses her
fingers. Then he raises his fingers to JEANNIE's lips.*

Suddenly, comprehension dawns. She takes his fingers, gently raises them to her lips and kisses the cut.)

GORDONOV: Now we'll just have to wait and see.

JEANNIE: You're sure you wanted to do this?

GORDONOV: I'm sure.

JEANNIE: How will you know?

GORDONOV: My flying. If it works, I won't be able to fly.

JEANNIE: You're willing to give up so much.

GORDONOV: What I'm gaining is more important. *(He pauses.)* I have no experience with this. But with Mother I don't think it took very long. Minutes, seconds.

JEANNIE: I mean that much to you?

GORDONOV: No, you mean more.

(He stands up as JEANNIE rushes toward him. They embrace, JEANNIE's back to the audience. As they break apart, we see that she has grown fangs.)

GORDONOV: My God!

JEANNIE: I had to be sure.

GORDONOV: Sure?

JEANNIE: That you really felt the same as my uncle and I do. I loved you, but there was that little bit of doubt.

GORDONOV: Doubt?

JEANNIE: Uncle Don and I thought we were the only vampires. We thought maybe if there were others, they were like the old legends. Bloodthirsty monsters.

GORDONOV: Your uncle?

JEANNIE: Of course, Jack. You said he saw you and knew what you were. *(Pause)* Of course, he did. Why else do you think he'd introduce me to a vampire?

(Curtain)

4. Analyze the script in much the same way you did with those in "Market." You won't need to go through so many steps since there are only two characters.

155

Unlike "Market," "Vampire" is light and playful. It is largely for fun, although the author still has something to say. What is the theme of the play? Why do you think so?

a. What is the relationship between Gordonov and Jeannie? How does Gordonov's view of the relationship differ from Jeannie's? Do you think she should let him go on thinking she was a human being for as long as she did? Why? How do they feel about each other? Why are they both hesitant about the relationship?

b. What type of person is Gordonov? Jeannie? Do you like them? Why? How are they different from human beings? How are they similar? Which side of them do you think is more important — human or vampire?

c. What conflict occurs in this play? Does it build? Where do the turning point and climax occur? Is this a reasonable solution? Why?

Directors sometimes have characters improvise scenes that are unrelated to the play. For instance, a director might ask the Old Man and Old Woman to improvise a scene where "the grandbabies" have just left and the two characters are straightening up the house. Or it may be something that is logical for them but not referred to in the play. An example might be to play a scene where you are getting ready to spend an evening with your best friends. Based on what you know of the characters, you then figure out the sorts of things they would say to each other and their attitudes and the mood each is in.

5. This is a four-part exercise.

a. Choose a partner of the opposite sex who will work with you on the last part of this exercise. Then choose characters (other than the jogger) from either "Market" or "Vampire" and analyze them, asking anything that is important. You can follow the categories suggested earlier: physical traits, background, attitudes and beliefs and patterns of behavior. Make sure you know your character as well as you can.

b. Write a character sketch of at least one page

describing the character you chose, using both traits and characteristics from the script and those you came up with that help fill out the character. Finish this for the next class meeting.

c. Tell your classmates which character you chose, and answer any questions they ask about that character. This is to make sure you do know as much as you can about him or her.

d. The following day your teacher will ask you to improvise a scene as the two characters you chose.

A good class project might be to come up with logical scenes for every set of characters to play.

157

Working With Original Characters

1. Apply what you learned about analyzing a character to an entirely different set of circumstances. Eavesdrop on a conversation at school or in a public place, such as a restaurant or store.

Keep as close a record of the conversation as you can. On the basis of what you heard and saw of the person, develop a character. Talk to the class for a minute as that character extending the conversation you heard between the two people. Then get together with someone else and come up with an improvisation scene involving your two characters.

2. Figure out what traits you most like in a friend. Develop a character based on these traits. Do the same thing with traits that you dislike. Now put the two characters who came from this into a one-minute scene that you outline. With a partner perform the scene, each of you basing your character on the traits.

3. Think of an emotion such as disgust. Now create a character who is disgusted for this reason. What does the person say and do? To whom is he or she speaking? Where are they? Describe the environment and the circumstances on paper. Then in a monolog that you improvise as you go along, play the character and tell the audience everything that happened when you felt disgusted.

Try the same thing with other emotions such as anger or jealousy.

THE CHARACTER INTERVIEW

There's an acting exercise called the character interview. It has three rules:

1. You cannot plan anything ahead of time.

2. You cannot answer as yourself but rather as a character who is beginning to take shape.

3. All the answers have to be consistent; there can be no contradictory traits.

A person agrees to be "it," and other actors ask questions.

Here's the way it works:

    Q. What's your name?

    A. Bill Johnson.

    Q. Where do you live?

    A. In San Diego.

    Q. What do you do there?

    A. Not much.

    Q: What do you mean?

    A. I mean I don't have a job.

    Q. Why not?

    A. It's none of your business, okay? All right. I flunked out of school, and my dad kicked me out. I can't find no job or nothin'.

    Q. What would you like to do?

    A: Be a brain surgeon! Get real, man.

    Q: How old are you, Bill?

A: I'm 19.

Q: So your dad kicked you out.

A: He didn't want me around anymore. So what the hell, if he didn't want me, I'll make it on my own.

Q: Sounds like you might be having a tough time of it.

A: You could say that. I've been sleeping on the beach. Begging people for money to eat. Just look at me. My clothes are filthy. I ain't got nothin'. And my pop. He's rich, man. Got a Mercedes and a BMW. Belongs to the country club. Raises money for all kinds of stuff. Just so long as it ain't for me.

Q: Have you tried to talk to your dad?

A: Ain't no use. You see, he ain't my real father. My real dad died when I was just a kid. Mom married this guy, and he didn't want to have nothin' to do with me.

Q: Won't your mom —

A: Mom's dead! An accident. Seems to me like it was his fault.

Q: Your stepfather's?

A: Yeah, but the cops wouldn't listen.

The idea is just to let the answers flow. It's a little like brainstorming or word association. Don't be afraid to say the first thing that comes into your head.

You can even ask yourself questions, if you want to. This is particularly useful if you're trying to learn about an existing character, one you're working on for a play. For instance:

Q: What's your name?

A: Jeannie.

Q: Where are you from, Jeannie?

A: Right now I live in San Diego.

Q: Right now? Where did you live before that?

A: All over the world.

Q: That must have been exciting.

A: I suppose. But I'd give anything to settle down.

Q: Why don't you?

A: I can't; I really can't. People would start asking too many questions.

Q: What do you mean?

A: Nothing. Oh, all right . . . It's just that my uncle and I can never stay too long in one place.

Q: Are you criminals or something?

A: Heavens no! Whatever gave you an idea like that?

Q: You said you have to move around.

A: That's right.

Q: How old are you, Jeannie?

A: I'm . . . a lot older than you think.

Q: How do you know what I think?

A: (Laughing) You think I'm in my 20s, I'll bet.

Q: I suppose so. Yeah, I do. How old are you?

A: About five hundred, I think.

Q: Whoa, wait a minute. How can that be?

A: I've never told this to anyone before, at least since I was a little girl. I'm a vampire.

Q: Sure you are.

4. Do a day of character interviews. Just let the answers flow. It's best if the questions and the answers are spontaneous. If you think of something to ask someone who's "it," for instance, just ask without waiting to be called on.

After your interview, take a few minutes to jot down everything you remember. Your teacher will tape each interview so that later, after all the interviews are finished, you can listen to it. As you do, write down anything important that you didn't remember.

Then get together with one of the other "characters." Get in front of the class and do an improvisational scene using one of the following situations. Even though the situations will be the same for all of you, the way the scene progresses and the outcome should be a lot different because of the sorts of people you'll be playing.

161

a. You are involved in a minor traffic accident when one of you is on the way to the airport to catch a plane; the other has an important meeting scheduled.

b. One of you has just been mugged and your money stolen. The other stops to help, but the victim thinks the other person is the mugger.

c. You are going to a party together and get lost. Each of you blames the other.

d. You've known each other for a long time, but never got along. Now you're trapped in an old house where you've both gone to escape an unexpected blizzard.

A character, whether it is one you developed or one that already exists, often suggests other characters, as well as additional action and situations. Character, situation and plot are the three essential parts of a play.

5. The following story sets up an unusual situation.

Break into groups of four or five. First, figure out what is happening and, on the basis of what is here, extend the story. You might want to bring in other characters such as Maria, but you don't have to. You can develop others who haven't been mentioned. Don't write it out in detail, but just plan the broad outline. Then as a group, present an improvisation based on what you've written. Since several groups will be working with this one story, there should be a big difference in what is presented.

The name of the story is "The Laughter," and it was written by Anne James Valades.

Five men stood in front of the aqueduct, under the outspread branches of an *amate* tree, their hands tied behind their backs.

Chente watched the men, waiting for the order to fire.

When he was a boy, the *amate* trees, here in the village of Chiconcuac, filled Chente with a sense of peace. They offered him comfort in a way nothing else could. He felt their giant presence watch over him like a guardian angel. Their branches had sheltered him from the hot noonday sun, and provided a hiding place when he wanted to escape his parents' vigilance.

But the year was 1912. Vicente "Chente" Ayala was 20 years old and had been with the Zapatista revolutionaries for 18 months. All he wanted now was to rest from the fighting and the killing, and to go home, to see his mother and father, his brothers and sisters, and . . . Maria.

You are already acquainted with word association. You can use this to develop a character. Start with a physical or personality trait, such as "arrogant" and continue with any other traits that come to mind. For example: arrogant, pudgy, tidy, sly, pale, perfectionist.

Write out 10 to 12 traits. Then take four or five and use them to write a character sketch. Add whatever you wish to what you already have.

For instance, Jack Oleson is 35 years old. His most outstanding trait is his *arrogance*. *Pale* and *pudgy,* he is almost ugly. Oddly enough, he never seems to lack female companionship. Yet, he's rarely seen with the same woman twice. He's *sly* enough to capture a woman's attention, but apparently too much of a *perfectionist* to put up with those who aren't as smart or rich as he.

If you wish, you can immediately place the character in a setting:

Jack Oleson, publisher of the *Cleveland Times,* sat at his desk, playing with an antique letter opener. Tonight he'd be going to the opera with Lucretia Smitley of the Cincinnati Smitleys. He certainly hoped she matched her reputation for brilliance. He was sick to the very core with stupid, senseless women who passed themselves off as intelligent. He glanced at the cuckoo clock on the far wall and decided to call her. His heart beat like thunder when someone answered and announced: "Lucretia Smitley is dead."

The idea, even when you begin the character sketch, is simply to let your imagination flow. Then you may want to decide on the reasons a person has certain traits. What caused Jack to become such a perfectionist? Maybe it was because his folks ridiculed him as a kid, telling him he couldn't measure up, couldn't be good at anything.

Maybe because of this, he really feels inferior instead of superior or arrogant. He tells himself that he's better than others but knows he isn't. At the same time, he subconsciously feels that the women he dates are better than he is, and he can't accept it, so he tells himself they're stupid.

You can build a character through word association either by yourself or with others.

6. Take turns listing either a physical or a personality trait until you have 10 or 12. Your teacher will list them on the chalkboard.

Then begin using them to build a character. Remember that you need only use four or five, and you can add whatever else you like. When you finish, read your character sketches to the class.

7. Work three in a group. Using your word association character sketch, think of a logical situation in which to place your character. This means placing the person with one or more of your classmates' characters. On the basis of what they're like, figure out what sort of conflict is logical. Talk about the improvisation you can do as a result of this. Set up the situation and the setting, and the next time the class meets present the scene.

8. In the following story called "Hate Child" by Art Specht, there is the potential for a lot of conflict. Work with two classmates, and extend this opening scene further to show what happens. Using the "facts" and clues the author provided, add traits to Charlie Bob's character; then figure out traits for "the voice." Decide who or what this is and why it is calling him. It might help to know that this is a horror story, and the voice the boy hears is trying to lure him to the shambles of an old house on a small island.

It was Sunday, the morning of my 12th birthday. My daddy was passed out in his hammock on the porch, his mouth hanging open, a half-drunk jar of shine underneath his hammock. A flock of flies had come through the punched-out window screens and was buzzing around his head, while the tip of his tongue poked out over his bottom lip like the end of an old yellow sponge. He'd clean forgot it was my birthday. He'd never even bought me a present like he'd used to do before my mama had passed away.

I was feeling awful sorry for myself, setting in that old wicker chair watching him. I recollected when my mama was alive on my ninth birthday, the big chocolate cake she'd made, how all them kids had come over and stuffed themselves with ice cream and cake and played pin-the-tail-on-the-donkey. I got all watery eyed. My mama had died in a car accident one month before my birthday.

I was thinking hard about her when all of a sudden I heard this voice whispering inside my head. The hair on my neck prickled and goose bumps jumped up all over me. I figured it was my mama talking to me from the grave. Then the voice came again, and I knew it wasn't her. It was a young gal's voice that I'd never heard before.

"Charlie Bob," she called, like she was a long distance away. "Come see me. I'm at the old Bordon house. Got a chocolate cake that I made special for your birthday."

It scared me, hearing someone talk inside my head that way, because I figured I might be catching one of them mental breakdowns . . .

"Charlie-Bob, did you hear me?" she called again, only a heap louder this time.

Popping straight up in my chair, I waved the flies away from my face and looked around, seeing if one of my friends had sneaked up on me . . . There wasn't nobody on the porch, except me and my daddy.

Lord, I'm sure enough hearing things, I thought.

[The voice keeps asking him to come to the island. He ignores it until two bullies attempt to beat him up.]

[Hambone] bent over to pull me to my feet. Just as his fingers closed around my arm, he screamed. A big crimson flower blossomed on the right side of his face, then wilted and poured off his chin. When I looked close I saw four deep gashes had laid open his cheek. A second later, Joe let out a godawful howl. It was like a phantom cleaver had hacked off the end of his nose. Blood squirted from the middle of his face and spilled on the sidewalk, making bright red splotches at his feet.

"You can come see me now," she said. "They won't bother you no more."

Lord, it shocked me spitless, seeing what she'd done to them two. My mouth flopped open while Hambone and Joe caterwauled, hands clamped to their bloody faces . . .

Try to come up with an ending that you think is logical. You can add whatever characters you like. But develop them through the word association method, keeping in mind that they have to fit in with what the story already says. Trade outlines with another group. On the basis of the new outline, you should present an improvisational scene showing what happens. If you need more people for your scene, ask those in other groups to help you out.

It's a lot easier to play people your own age or older. It might be a challenge to play a 12-year-old.

You can also begin by naming a single trait and building a character from it. You do the same thing as you did in asking why a person is a certain way and how it has affected him or her.

For example, suppose the first thing that comes to mind is "blind." Then you begin asking questions about this.

Why is the person blind? She was in an automobile accident.

When did the accident happen? When she was 18 years old.

How did it happen? Her brother was driving too fast on a winding road. He'd just bought his first car and was seeing how fast it would go.

How has the accident affected her life? For a long time she refused to do anything except stay in her room. She'd been in college, with the goal of becoming an architect.

How old is she now? Twenty.

What is her name? Sally Thomas.

What is she doing? She takes care of her brother whose spinal cord was severed in the accident and who is confined to a wheelchair.

How does she feel about that? For a long time she was glad he was paralyzed. But then she relented. Now she can't forgive herself for the feelings.

How do they live? The family provides an allowance.

Why don't they live with their parents? Their mother and father are divorced and remarried. Because she was so bitter about what happened, she refused to stay with either parent. Her brother decided to stay with her — with an attendant for the first year — because he apparently felt he had to do some sort of penance for making her blind. He's a year younger than she is.

Of course, you can go on with this as long as you like, until you feel both a character and a situation are emerging. It often happens that one character will suggest another. Here it was the brother. Then too there was the attendant, hired to take care of the brother.

As you see, this is a combination of word association and the character interview.

Another thing you can figure out about a character you develop completely on your own or that is based on another character is the *dominant trait*. This is the most important trait, at least in terms of the improvisation.

For example, Sally's dominant trait could be "shame" at how she hated her brother. So everything she does now is to make it up to him for the way she felt. So she is overly-solicitous, fussing over him as if he's incapable of doing anything to help himself. She constantly asks him if he's eaten all his food, if he's comfortable, if he's too warm or too cold, if he wants anything. He now is the one who begins building up a resentment, which gradually becomes his dominant trait — affecting everything he does or says. He even comes to believe that Sally won't leave him alone for even a second because it's her way of getting revenge.

When he snaps at her or becomes disagreeable, she tries even harder to make sure even the tiniest things are to his liking. This then is what causes the conflict.

9. Look again at "Market" or "Vampire." What do you think are the major character's dominant traits? What drives them to act as they do? Discuss this with the rest of the class and try to come to an agreement.

It's possible that actors' ideas of the dominant trait will differ. For instance, in "Market," Jimmy's dominant trait might be impatience. He's impatient with everyone who doesn't fit in with his idea of what people should be like. So he makes fun of everyone. Or his dominant trait could be that he's unfeeling, and so it amuses him to make fun of everyone.

The reason for figuring out a character's dominant trait is that in an improvisation of only several minutes or even a play of two hours, there isn't time to deal with the whole personality of any one character. So you pick out the most important traits and explore them for an audience.

The dominant traits are tied in with the character's goals and intentions. Sally Thomas' goal is to make sure her brother is well taken care of; this is because of her guilt. Her intention behind this is to ease her own guilt.

10. With a partner, develop two characters by starting with a single trait. One character may remind you of another. Figure out their relationship with each other, their dominant traits and then how the traits are tied in with goals or intentions. How are these goals or intentions in conflict? For example, Sally wants to take care of her brother; the brother wants to be left alone.

Once you figure out all these things, present an improvisational scene showing the two characters in conflict.

You can use a number of other ways to begin building characters, a scene and conflict. You already have done some improvisation with objects and photos. You can also use drawings.

These two drawings by Gene Gryniewicz depict strong feelings of tension and conflict.

11. Divide into groups of three or four and work out an improvisational scene based on the silhouette. You might begin by asking yourselves such questions as:

a. Why is someone standing under the lamp post?
b. Who is he?
c. What sort of person is he?
d. What is he planning?
e. Who else is involved?
f. Who is going to be affected by this?
g. He looks sinister. Why?

You can keep going with questions until you have characters, a particular scene and conflict.

Next work out an outline and an improvisational scene of about five minutes that involves everyone in your group.

12. Once more divide into groups, but with a different combination of people. Now use the drawing of the woman as the basis for a scene. Begin with such questions as:

    a. Where is she?

    b. Who is she?

    c. Why is she behind barbed wire?

    d. Is she waiting for someone?

    e. If so, who is it?

    f. What are they going to do?

As you did with the other drawing, figure out a scene that you can improvise, using all the members of your group. This scene also should last about five minutes.

13. Choose the character you developed through one basic trait, through word association or with the character interview.

Now play the "what if" game.

For instance, what if someone kidnapped Sally Thomas and held her for ransom? What if her brother — whose name is Ben — decided he really did love her and had been letting petty resentments get in the way? What if he decided to rescue Sally?

Or what if Jack Oleson, while in the middle of a blackout, did try to kill Lucretia Smitley? Although they hadn't met before, what if he was afraid that she was more intelligent and capable than he? And what if she really wasn't dead, but the person who answered the phone in some way was trying to trap Jack? And what if Jack suddenly remembers the period in which he blacked out and realizes he did "kill" Lucretia. And what if Lucretia has strange powers that keep her from being killed? And what if she now comes after Jack? And what if this all is a plot to gain control of his newspaper? And what if the reason she wants to gain control is so that . . .

You can keep going with this until an entire set of characters and an entire plot suggests itself. Then make an outline of the plot and with others in the class present an improvisational scene showing what happens.

As you learned earlier, there are always intentions behind each goal. Lucretia may want to gain control of the paper simply because she hates Jack and wants to destroy him. Or she may want to gain control of the paper because she wants to have a way of spreading her views that her "people" are the only ones capable of running the planet. Or she may want to give the paper to her boyfriend, an extra-terrestrial alien like herself, so that he has a way of making money to buy the necessary material to fuel their ship for its flight home. You could go on and on with intentions. Of course, if you were going to play one of these two characters, deciding on the intention behind the actions would make a difference in how you present the person.

In scenes or plays that are longer than a few minutes, the characters may have one overall intention in reaching a particular goal, but different minor intentions in each scene. These minor intentions contribute to the overall intention.

For instance in "Vampire," Jeannie's overall intention is to spend her life with Gordonov. But she holds back and allows him to tell her he is a vampire. Her intention here is to see if his views are the same as hers and her uncle's. The reason, as she says, is that she and her uncle know nothing about other vampires.

Intention is the part of a play that rarely is stated, but is the reason behind everything a character does.

14. What do you think are the goals and overall intentions in the following? The story is "Coffee Cure-All," and it was written by Nirmala Moorthy.

> "Letter from Los Angeles," he says, tossing the envelope on the coffee table as he comes in the front door. He is already loosening his tie and wriggling free of his jacket. It's like any other evening in April. I have no premonition of the storm cloud that looms on the horizon. Not so much as an inkling of the twister that waits to lift and whirl and slam us down, with little regard to how we fall.
>
> My husband is never vocal when he comes home from work. He needs a drink and a shower before he can find the energy to talk. Tom's company deals in microchips and disk drives. They have their headquarters in Los Angeles. He manages the Japan sector, and

has a modest office in Tokyo's Maranouchi district.

"Chicken's delicious," he says, as we sit across the supper table. "Tell me about your day." Good, he's human again. We can talk. "I've read the letter from L.A.," I say. "Did you call the head office, Tom? When exactly is he coming?"

"Day after tomorrow." Tom looks at me warily, and I know there's worse to come.

"Two days? Couldn't he have given you some time to prepare?"

"He could have, but he didn't. That's his usual style. He likes to catch people unprepared."

"How about a hotel booking?" There's a long moment of silence. I can guess what's coming.

"Another two weeks and it'll be cherry blossom time, honey. Have you forgotten what it's like this time of year? We'll be swamped with tourists."

"Is he coming only to see the sakura trees?" My question is pertinent because a lot of Japanese do just that. Sakura viewing is taken seriously in Japan, and offices declare holidays when the trees are in full bloom. Crowds flock to the Imperial Palace or Shinjuku gardens to have sake parties. They carry little portable burners to heat the wine, and have a rollicking time. "Don't say all the hotels in town are booked up, Tom?"

"You said it," he says. "Tokyo's where it's all happening, honey. There are three international conferences scheduled for next week, and my guess is he wants to attend all of them."

"And . . .?"

"And we can't put him in a ryokan — they say he's very fussy. He's just the type to insist on a ryokan as the ultimate Japanese experience, and then complain about the lack of 'western' amenities. Honey, I'm sorry but we'll have to put him up here." Ryokans are Japanese inns. Although they are pretty and expensive, they are uncomfortable for "fussy" people. Bathing facilities have to be shared, and the guest sleeps on a futon, a mattress, which rolls up and sits in a cupboard during the day.

"Here?" We live in a quaint Japanese house with tatami mats, sliding walls, and paper screens in the windows. You can't breathe without being heard in the next room. I love it dearly, but it can never compare with the Hilton. "The maid service here might not measure up to his expectations, Tom."

"But we have the best chef in town," says Tom. Flattery always gets him somewhere. "That's all that matters. A little extra work for all of us, honey, but it's only for a few weeks."

"A few weeks!"

"Two weeks," says Tom, "but what's the alternative? One false move and my career is a clod of mud. He's the president of the company. He's used to being difficult, and getting away with it." An offer I can't refuse. It is decided. Sam Hudson will stay with us.

The day of his arrival dawns bright and clear, and I stifle my misgivings. As he comes down the ramp and into the "immigration" area of Narita International, I get a good look at him from the gallery. He looks more like Kitanoumi, my favorite Sumo wrestler, than a business executive. His pot obstructs my views of his feet. I guess that he walks with short, quick steps for he moves fast. He rolls smoothly into the arrival lounge. The glare from the tube lights bounces off his top, and defines the thick half-moon of slicked-down hair that stretches from ear to ear. His trim moustache, bright blue eyes, and concentric chins create an aura of comic good humor. His grey woolen suit looks expensive, but slightly creased now after a nine-hour flight from Los Angeles. He is first off the plane, and first to come out of "immigration" and "customs." Obviously a man who pushes himself to the forefront and gets things done.

The official grapevine has not deceived us. Sam Hudson appreciates comfort. A fleeting look of dismay cramps his face when Tom shows him our guest room.

In Tokyo, where land is scarcer and more expensive than Manhattan, houses are scaled down to people-size. Although not a tall man, Sam Hudson has three times the girth of the average Japanese. The twinkle dies in those shrewd blue eyes when he visits our bathroom for the first time. We have an excellently designed Japanese bath. Which means that the architect has put the minimum space to optimum use. Apparently there's not enough room for Sam to move around comfortably.

"I had to come out in reverse gear," he tells us. "And there's no way you're going to get me to climb into your little square tub."

"I like him," I say to Tom later that night. "He has a sense of humor."

"Instant coffee!" says Sam, the third evening when I serve it after supper. The revelation shocks him to the extent that he drops the cup, and ruins my Chinese embroidered tablecloth. "Nobody drinks instant coffee," he says, when he recovers slightly.

Since his arrival we have fallen head-first into a vortex of activity that continues unabated for two weeks. Sam Hudson certainly gets his money's worth from his employees. My husband spends at least twelve hours a day steering his boss through discussions and meetings with top Japanese executives. Soon Tom's extra-large frame is wearing out at the edges. His black hair looks straggly, his beard bristles. But his nerves are resilient, like India rubber.

"Careful, Susan," I say to myself. "Stick with it, girl! Another ten days, and it'll be over." I go about my work, silently simmering, while they discuss microprocessors and cash-flow projections. And litter the coffee table with graphs and charts. I zip from room to room at lightning speed, dishing out hot breakfasts and business lunches, juggling the baby, the laundry, the lessons in Judo and Japanese.

"Oh, for some time to breathe!" I tell Tom. Sam Hudson carries on, blissfully unaware.

Our guest's habit of drinking about twelve cups of

coffee per day adds to the chaos. Tom and I do drink coffee. We also drink tea, Japanese tea, or any other hot drink that warms the throat on a cold day. To us, coffee is just another drink. To Sam Hudson, the drinking of coffee constitutes a sacred rite, not to be undertaken in a spirit of levity. He approaches the matter with the devotion of an acolyte and worse — he expects us to do the same.

15. Do one of the following:

a. Take Sam from "Coffee Cure-All" and the Old Woman from "Market." Do an improvisational scene of three to four minutes in which she invites him to her house for a cup of coffee.

b. Put Tom from "Coffee Cure-All" and Jimmy from "Market" and Gordonov from "Vampire" together in a scene where they talk about the elderly.

c. Take Jeannie from "Vampire," Velda from "Market" and Susan from "Coffee Cure-All" and have them confront the Old Woman about the way she treats the Old Man.

GIVEN CIRCUMSTANCES

Given circumstances include any background information necessary for understanding a play. It is sometimes called the *exposition* and includes such things as the setting, the time period, the economic conditions of the characters and the world, and background information on the characters.

The background or given circumstances for improvisations usually isn't as complete. But the better it's worked out, the better the chance that the improvisation will work well. For instance:

Setting: An alley in the middle of a city, late at night.

Characters: A young woman whose car has broken down. A young man who approaches her.

Action: The woman is frantically looking for a pay phone; the young man approaches her and demands she come with him. She tries to run.

175

There can be many intentions. For instance:

a. The man may want to rob her; she may be frantically trying to escape.

b. He may be her husband who is just getting off work and has asked her to have the car fixed before it breaks down. She may be trying to escape because she knows he has a terrible temper.

c. The young man is her fiance; she came to tell him she was breaking off the engagement, and now her car won't start. He wants to help her, but she thinks he'll try to talk her out of it before she can get away.

Or take a different situation:

Setting: The living room of a middle-class house.

Characters: Bob and Joy Randall.

Action: A woman nagging her husband to take her out to dinner. He doesn't want to go.

Various intentions:

a. The woman is planning a surprise birthday party for Bob, her husband. Bob is tired after working all day and has expected to come home to a relaxing dinner. She has to get him out of the house so the guests can sneak in.

b. Bob is reneging on his promise to take his young wife Joy out to dinner and then a show. They've been married only a few months, and he's embarrassed to tell her he forgot to buy the tickets, so he's pretending he doesn't feel like going.

c. The doctor has told Bob, who's had a serious illness, that he has to get active again, so Joy wants to help him. He feels that he's going to die and there's no point in doing anything.

d. Joy and Bob are brother and sister. Bob has come for a visit and is tired after a long flight. Joy has arranged for him to meet her best friends. He wants to meet them, but later, because he feels he wouldn't be good company.

You could go on with many different intentions.

16. Often a director will privately tell each performer his intention for an improvisational scene without letting the others know what it is. Remember that there can be many different intentions for any particular role. Your teacher will do that with the following, which you should then present in a three- to four-minute improvisation.

    a. Setting: A street corner, early afternoon, summer.

       Characters: A man and woman in their early 20s, casually dressed.

       Action: The man is standing on the sidewalk tapping his foot. He demands that she join him. She refuses.

    b. Setting: The sidewalk in front of a store window.

       Characters: Two girls of high school age.

       Action: One of the girls is trying to pull the other into the store.

    c. Setting: An area around one of the benches in a city park.

       Characters: Three boys and two girls, all juniors and seniors in high school.

       Action: The boys demand the girls come with them; the girls refuse.

17. Each person should come up with one set of given circumstances and at least five sets of intentions for each. Each then will have the chance to choose cast members and tell them their intentions.

Often when you begin with a character, no matter whether the person is developed through the interview method, the word association method or any other way, you sometimes can build this into an entire play.

18. Take one of the characters you have developed, or that is from this chapter. Working together as a class, begin improvising further scenes with the idea of developing this into a one-act play of 20 to 30 minutes. Figure out what sort of conflict the person would have, what his or her most important goal is. Be sure to spend enough time and effort for as long as it takes to come up with something you like. Be prepared to spend at least two weeks. Once the play is pretty well set in outline, you can keep

going over it and improving it.

After the same scene is presented a number of times, you may want to begin writing down dialog. Of course, this depends on the amount of time you have to work with the play.

ABOUT THE AUTHOR

Dr. Marsh Cassady has taught theatre at the high school and college levels for many years. He is currently a director, actor and award-winning free-lance writer. He received both his M.A. and his Ph.D. from Kent State University. He has conducted many workshops on playwriting and has directed and acted in more than 100 plays. Additionally, he has been a columnist, book reviewer, and dramatic writer for radio shows. His list of more than 20 books on various theatre arts is widely used in schools in the United States and Canada.

If you enjoyed
Acting Games
you'll like this other
Meriwether Publishing
book of
improvisational
exercises:

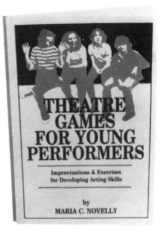

THEATRE GAMES FOR YOUNG PERFORMERS

by MARIA C. NOVELLY

Written especially for adolescent actors, this delightfully fresh workbook tells you the how, when, what and why of theatre games. Anyone working with young actors in schools or recreational centers will find this book exceptionally helpful. The basics of pantomime, improvisations, voice control, monologs and dialogs are all presented in game formats with exercises and worksheets for easy organization.

This paperback book is available at bookstores or from Meriwether Publishing Ltd., P.O. Box 7710, Colorado Springs, Colorado 80933.

Paperback book (160 pages) ISBN 0-916260-31-3

ORDER FORM

MERIWETHER PUBLISHING LTD.
P.O. BOX 7710
COLORADO SPRINGS, CO 80933
TELEPHONE: (719) 594-4422

Please send me the following books:

_____ **Acting Games — Improvisations and**   **$14.95**
Exercises #TT-B168
by Marsh Cassady
A textbook of theatre games and improvisations

_____ **Theatre Games for Young Performers #TT-B188**   **$14.95**
by Maria C. Novelly
Improvisations and exercises for developing acting skills

_____ **Improve With Improv! #TT-B160**   **$12.95**
by Brie Jones
A guide to improvisation and character development

_____ **Improvisations in Creative Drama #TT-B138**   **$12.95**
by Betty Keller
A collection of improvisational exercises and sketches for acting students

_____ **Truth in Comedy #TT-B164**   **$14.95**
by Charna Halpern, Del Close and Kim "Howard" Johnson
The manual of improvisation

_____ **Winning Monologs for Young Actors #TT-B127**   **$14.95**
by Peg Kehret
Honest-to-life monologs for young actors

_____ **Everything About Theatre! #TT-B200**   **$16.95**
by Robert L. Lee
The guidebook of theatre fundamentals

**These and other fine Meriwether Publishing books are available at
your local bookstore or direct from the publisher. Use the handy
order form on this page.**

NAME: _____

ORGANIZATION NAME: _____

ADDRESS: _____

CITY: _____ STATE: _____

ZIP: _____ PHONE: _____

    ❑ **Check Enclosed**
    ❑ **Visa or MasterCard #** _____

                                       Expiration
Signature: _____ *Date:* _____
         (required for Visa/MasterCard orders)

COLORADO RESIDENTS: Please add 3% sales tax.
SHIPPING: Include $2.75 for the first book and 50¢ for each additional book ordered.

    ❑ *Please send me a copy of your complete catalog of books and plays.*